Antalya Travel Guide 2023-2024

The Gateway to Turkey's Turquoise Coast

Bruce Terry

Bruce Terry

Copyright © 2023 Bruce Terry All rights reserved.

No part of this book may be reproduced, stored in a retrieval system, or transmitted in any form or by any means electronic, mechanical, photocopying, recording, scanning, or otherwise without the prior written permission of the publisher.

The work contained herein is the sole property of the author and may not be reproduced or copied in any form without express permission from the author. All information is provided as is, without any warranty of any kind, liability expressly disclaimed. The publisher and the author disclaim any liability for any loss, risk, or damage allegedly arising from the use, application, or interpretation of the content herein.

Bruce Terry

MAP OF ANTALYA

Bruce Terry

Bruce Terry

TABLE OF CONTENTS

MAP OF ANTALYA 3

INTRODUCTION 9

    HISTORY 11

    WEATHER AND CLIMATE... 13

    10 REASONS WHY YOU SHOULD VISIT ANTALYA 15

CHAPTER 1 19

    GENERAL INFORMATION 19

    • POPULATION 19

    PUBLIC HOLIDAY 21

    ELECTRIC PLUG 24

    CURRENCY 26

    LANGUAGE 29

    VISA REQUIREMENT 32

    DIETARY RESTRICTIONS AND EATING 35

    CYBER CAFES 38

    LOCAL TIME 41

CHAPTER 2 47

    BEST TIME TO VISIT ANTALYA 47

    MONEY SAVING TIPS... 49

CHAPTER 3 53

GETTING AROUND ANTALYA 53

HOW TO GET FROM ANTALYA AIRPORT TO CITY CENTER 57

HOW TO GET FROM ANTALYA AIRPORT TO THE NEAREST HOTELS 59

PUBLIC WIFI AVAILABILITY IN ANTALYA 61

Free Public WiFi Hotspots: 61

Antalya Municipality WiFi: 62

CHAPTER 4 65

WHAT YOU NEED TO PACK ON A TRIP TO ANTALYA 65

- WHAT TO PACK FOR WINTER 65
- WHAT TO PACK FOR SPRING 68
- WHAT TO PACK FOR SUMMER 71
- WHAT TO PACK FOR AUTUMN 73

CHAPTER 5 77

TOP TOURIST DESTINATIONS IN ANTALYA 77

Kaleici (Old Town): 77

Antalya Museum: 77

Aspendos: 77

CHAPTER 6 81

BEST BEACHES IN ANTALYA 81

BEST RESTAURANTS IN ANTALYA 84

BUDGET-FRIENDLY HOTELS IN ANTALYA 87

BEST LUXURY HOTELS IN ANTALYA 90

BEST SHOPPING MALLS IN ANTALYA 93

BEST MUSEUMS IN ANTALYA 96

BEST PARKS AND GARDENS IN ANTALYA 99

BEST NIGHTCLUBS AND BARS IN ANTALYA 102

NIGHTLIFE IN ANTALYA 105

- LIVE MUSIC 105
- ROMANTIC EVENING 108

HEALTH AND SAFETY 110

PHARMACY AND FIRST AID 113

CHAPTER 7 117

FOOD AND DRINK 117

- LOCAL DRINKS 117
- STREET FOODS 119

CONCLUSION 121

Bruce Terry

Bruce Terry

INTRODUCTION

Welcome to Antalya, an exquisite city where ancient history meets contemporary luxury and beautiful beaches meet stunning natural scenery. Allow our thorough Antalya travel guide for 2023-2024 to be your compass as you commence your trip through this colorful coastal treasure, revealing the delights that await you.

Antalya, nestled amid the sun-kissed beaches of the Turkish Riviera, is a tribute to the region's rich historical legacy dating back thousands of years. Its history dates back to antiquity when it was a bustling port city for civilizations such as the Greeks, Romans, and Byzantines. Today, with its alluring blend of historical buildings, lively culture, and unrivaled natural beauty, this seaside paradise entices visitors from all over the globe.

Wander through the small, cobblestone alleyways of Antalya's charming Old Town, Kaleiçi, and immerse yourself in the heart of the city's history. Admire the well-preserved Roman structures, such as Hadrian's Gate, which has stood bravely for almost 1,800 years. Discover the awe-inspiring treasures of Antalya Museum, which houses an exceptional collection of items from the city's history.

Antalya's attractiveness goes beyond its historical significance. Soak up the sun on one of the region's gorgeous beaches, where blue seas caress golden dunes. From the renowned Konyaalt Beach to the

Bruce Terry

beautiful Lara Beach, these coastal havens are ideal for relaxation and rejuvenation.

The beautiful scenery that surrounds Antalya will fascinate nature lovers. Explore the unearthly splendor of the Saklikent Gorge, a natural marvel with towering cliffs and icy-cold streams. Explore the serene Düden Waterfalls, where falling waters crash into a crystal-clear pool, producing a breathtaking scene.

Aside from its historical riches and natural marvels, Antalya has a vibrant food industry that will excite your taste senses. Savor the pleasures of classic Turkish food, from scrumptious kebabs to exquisite baklava, on a gastronomic trip. Stroll through bustling marketplaces like the Kaleiçi Bazaar, smelling exotic spices and fresh vegetables, and adding a sensory layer to your Antalya experience.

As you tour the city, you'll come across a plethora of opulent resorts, boutique hotels, and lovely guesthouses that cater to the needs of every visitor. Antalya's broad choice of lodgings assures a wonderful stay, whether you choose a calm retreat, a family-friendly paradise, or a busy entertainment scene.

Prepare to embark on an incredible trip as you explore Antalya's treasures. Allow our Antalya travel guide for 2023-2024 to be your trusty companion as you discover the hidden jewels, must-see sights, and amazing experiences that await you in this seaside paradise. Discover Antalya's charm, where ancient history meets contemporary magnificence, and make memories that last a lifetime.

HISTORY

ancient and Ancient Times: The Antalya region has been inhabited since ancient times, with archaeological evidence indicating that it was originally colonized as early as the Paleolithic age. The finding of prehistoric tools and artifacts in neighboring caverns sheds light on the region's early human existence. Various ancient civilizations affected the area throughout time, notably the Hittites, who ruled the region circa 1500 BCE.

The area was influenced by the Lycians, an ancient Anatolian civilization notable for their unique language and rich cultural history, around the first millennium BCE. The Lycians founded many coastal cities, notably Xanthos, Patara, and Myra. These towns prospered as prominent trading hubs and played a vital part in Mediterranean marine commerce.

The province was conquered by the Persian Empire in the fourth century BCE, but it recovered its freedom with the advent of Alexander the Great. After Alexander's death, Antalya and its environs were included in the Kingdom of Pergamon, and eventually the Roman Republic.

Bruce Terry

During the Roman and Byzantine periods, Antalya, known as Attaleia at the time, prospered as an important port and trading hub. The Romans built major constructions such as Hadrian's Gate, a triumphal arch dedicated to the Roman Emperor Hadrian, and the spectacular Aspendos Theater, which is one of the world's best-preserved ancient theaters.

With the split of the Roman Empire in the fourth century CE, Antalya became part of the Byzantine Empire. During the 7th and 8th centuries, the city was critical in defending Byzantium from Arab invasions. During this time, the spectacular walls that encircle the ancient city were erected to guard against prospective invasions.

The Seljuk Turks, a strong Turkic dynasty, invaded Antalya in the 11th century and included it in their growing empire. With the building of beautiful mosques, medreses (theological schools), and caravanserais, the Seljuk Sultanate of Rum ushered in a new era of affluence in the area. The most famous example is Antalya's Yivli Minaret, which dates back to the 13th century.

The city was ruled by the Anatolian beylik of Teke, a Turkmen principality, in the early 14th century. The Teke beylik's rule, however, was short-lived, since the growing Ottoman Empire, led by Sultan Mehmed the Conqueror, and seized Antalya in 1391. The Ottoman era gave stability and growth to the city, and it grew into a prominent trading and agricultural hub.

Modern Antalya: After the Ottoman Empire fell apart in the early twentieth century, Antalya saw substantial transformations. Under the visionary leadership of Mustafa Kemal Atatürk, it became a part of the newly founded Republic of Turkey in 1923. Antalya evolved into a modern metropolis during the next several decades, with the expansion of infrastructure, tourism, and industry.

Antalya is already well-known as a popular tourist resort, receiving millions of people each year. Its beautiful beaches, historical attractions, and lively culture attract visitors from all over the globe. Rapid urbanization and economic expansion have also occurred in the city, with contemporary facilities and foreign hotels dotting the landscape.

WEATHER AND CLIMATE

a. *Spring (March to May):* Antalya's spring is pleasant and gentle, with temperatures gradually increasing from the chill of winter. In March, average daily temperatures vary from 15°C (59°F) to 23°C (73°F) in May. During this season, the city receives moderate rainfall, which makes the landscapes lush and vivid.

b. *Summer (June to August):* The summer in Antalya is hot and dry, with lots of sunlight. Temperatures may reach 30-35°C (86-95°F) on average, peaking in July and August. The cool air from the sea gives some reprieve from the heat. This is the busiest tourism season, with people flocking to beaches and resorts.

Bruce Terry

c. *Autumn (September to November):* Autumn in Antalya is pleasant and mild, with temperatures progressively decreasing. Summer-like weather persists in September, with average temperatures of about 28°C (82°F), while November marks the changeover to winter, with average temperatures of around 18°C (64°F). It's a terrific opportunity to see the city sans people.

d. *Winter (December to February):* Winters in Antalya are pleasant, with just a little rain on occasion. Temperatures in December vary from 11°C (52°F) to 15°C (59°F) in February. Snowfall is uncommon in the city, although the surrounding Taurus Mountains often get a dusting, providing a magnificent background.

Antalya gets the majority of its rainfall throughout the winter months. The city receives an average of 1,000 millimeters (39 inches) of precipitation every year, with December being the wettest month. Summer months, on the other hand, are rather dry, with minimal rain. The dry summers, along with the high temperatures, provide a classic Mediterranean climate.

Sunshine and daylight hours: Antalya is blessed with plenty of sunshine all year. The city receives over 3,000 hours of sunlight each year, making it one of the sunniest in Turkey. Summer days are lengthy, with up to 14 hours of daylight, giving plenty of time for outdoor activities and exploration.

Bruce Terry

Sea Temperature: Throughout the summer and into early fall, the Mediterranean Sea near Antalya maintains a suitable temperature for swimming. The sea temperature fluctuates from 24°C (75°F) to 28°C (82°F) from June to September, making it suitable for water-based sports and beach relaxation.

The Taurus Mountains, which are situated to the north of Antalya, have a considerable influence on the region's climate. They provide a microclimate by acting as a natural barrier, protecting the city from chilly winds. The mountains add to the lush flora, particularly during the rainy season, and provide a beautiful background for the coastal districts.

Understanding Antalya's weather and climate is essential for planning your activities and preparing properly. Antalya has something for everyone, whether you like the scorching and dry summers for beach lazing or the moderate and pleasant temps of spring and fall for touring the city's ancient landmarks. So pack your luggage and prepare to be enchanted by the splendor of this Mediterranean treasure!

10 REASONS WHY YOU SHOULD VISIT ANTALYA

Altalya has a rich historical legacy that extends back thousands of years. The ancient Greeks created the city, which has been affected by several civilizations, including the Romans, Byzantines, and Ottomans. Explore Hadrian's Gate, the old Aspendos Theater, and the Kaleici area, where you may meander through small alleyways dotted with Ottoman-era residences.

Stunning Beaches: One of Altalya's biggest charms is its magnificent coastline. The city is well-known for its beautiful beaches and crystal-clear seas. There is a beach to suit every taste, from the renowned Konyaalti Beach, with its vast expanse of golden sand, to the isolated Kaputas Beach, nestled away between towering rocks. Relax in the warm Mediterranean sun or participate in water activities like swimming, snorkeling, and diving.

Spectacular Landscapes: The natural beauty of Altaya goes beyond its shoreline. The area is home to a variety of sceneries that will captivate nature lovers. Visit the breathtaking Duden Waterfalls, where cascading waters crash into the sea, producing a captivating scene. Discover the stunning Taurus Mountains, which provide scenic hiking paths and panoramic views of the city and the Mediterranean.

Turkish Cuisine: Foodies will be delighted by Altalya's rich and delectable food scene. Traditional Turkish foods such as kebabs, mezes, and baklava are available. Visit the lively local markets, such as the Kaleici Bazaar, to experience a variety of fresh fruits, spices, and traditional delights. Don't forget to have a cup of Turkish tea or coffee while admiring the city's breathtaking sights.

Bruce Terry

Antalya has a Mediterranean climate, with long, hot summers and moderate winters. As a result, it is a perfect place for anyone looking for a bright and pleasant getaway. Altalya's comfortable temperature provides an excellent experience throughout the year, whether you wish to relax on the beach, tour historical monuments, or indulge in outdoor sports.

Altalya comes alive at night, providing a bustling and diversified entertainment environment. There is something for everyone, from sophisticated rooftop bars overlooking the Mediterranean to vibrant nightclubs catering to all tastes. Enjoy live music, dance the night away, or just unwind with a cool beverage while taking in the dynamic environment of the city.

Altalya has a variety of retail opportunities for individuals who like shopping. Explore sophisticated retail complexes such as TerraCity or MarkAntalya, which include both local and international brands. Wander through Kaleici's small alleyways, which are dotted with quaint boutiques, art galleries, and traditional Turkish artisan stores where you may buy one-of-a-kind treasures to take home.

Warmth & Hospitality: The inhabitants of Altalya are well-known for their warm hospitality and friendly demeanor. As you connect with the people, you will encounter true Turkish hospitality, as they are always willing to assist and share their culture. Whether it's starting up a discussion with a shopkeeper, sharing a typical Turkish dinner with a local family, or taking part in a cultural event, the people's friendliness will leave an indelible impression.

Proximity to the Antalya area: Altalya is an ideal starting point for exploring the larger Antalya area. Visit the historic city of Perge, the lovely seaside town of Kas, or the spectacular white travertine terraces of Pamukkale on day outings. Altalya's central position and well-connected transit make exploring the region's numerous offers simple.

Cultural Festivals and Events: Altalya holds a number of cultural festivals and events throughout the year that highlight the city's colorful legacy. There is always something going on in Altalya, from international music festivals to traditional dance performances and art exhibits. Immerse yourself in the local culture, observe traditional rituals, and join the people in celebrating during these festive events.

CHAPTER 1

GENERAL INFORMATION

POPULATION

Historical background: Understanding Altalya's population requires an examination of its historical background. Altalya has a long history, with influences from numerous civilizations including the ancient Altagradians, Byzantines, and Ottomans. These broad cultural exchanges have influenced the city's demography throughout time, drawing settlers and migrants from other places.

Current Population: According to the most recent available statistics in 2023, the population of Altalya is roughly 2.5 million people. The city has seen a significant population increase in recent decades, owing mostly to its strategic position, excellent climate, and solid economic possibilities. Altalya has developed into a commercial, tourist, and industrial center, drawing both local and foreign migrants.

Altalya has a diversified population makeup, which reflects the city's rich cultural past. Individuals from diverse ethnic origins, including Altagradians, Turks, Greeks, Armenians, and other minority groups, make up the population. This diversified environment has contributed to the city's dynamic climate, developing an inclusive and tolerant mentality.

Bruce Terry

Age Distribution: Altalya's population age distribution indicates a generally balanced profile. The city has a diverse age range, spanning from young toddlers to elderly people. The younger age accounts for a sizable proportion, owing to Altalya's reputation as an appealing location for young professionals, students, and families looking for better possibilities.

Variables Influencing Population Growth: Altalya's population growth has been influenced by a number of variables. Here are some significant players:

Economic Opportunities: Altalya's booming economy has attracted both local and foreign migrants. The city attracts persons looking for improved career chances by providing a variety of employment options in industries like as tourism, commerce, finance, and technology.

Tourism and Hospitality: Altalya is a famous tourist destination due to its natural beauty, historical landmarks, and cultural attractions. Tourism has surged in recent years, resulting in greater investment, infrastructure development, and job possibilities. Many people opt to live in Altalya after falling in love with the city during a visit.

Antalya is home to major educational institutions, like universities, research institutes, and schools. Students and academics from throughout the nation and beyond have been drawn to the availability of high-quality education and research possibilities.

Infrastructure Development: Altalya's infrastructure development, which includes transportation networks, healthcare facilities, and housing complexes, has played an important role in luring people to the city. Because of the government's efforts to establish a sustainable and pleasant urban environment, it has become an enticing location to live.

Population Density and Urban Planning: The population density in Altalya varies by neighborhood and district. To accommodate the city's rising population, the city has seen urban growth and the building of new residential districts. Initiatives in urban planning are focused on establishing well-designed neighborhoods, maintaining open areas, and guaranteeing appropriate infrastructure to fulfill inhabitants' needs.

PUBLIC HOLIDAY

Understanding Public Holidays: In Antalya, public holidays are national or religious holidays that are legally recognized by the Turkish government. These holidays usually include a day off from work or school, enabling both residents and visitors to participate in special activities and celebrations. Understanding the public holiday calendar can assist you in better planning your vacation and ensuring that you do not miss out on the unique experiences that these holidays provide.

Bruce Terry

Antalya's Major Public Holidays: 2.1 New Year's Day (January 1st): Antalya begins the year with a boom as residents and tourists celebrate New Year's Day. The city is decked up in festive decorations, and other activities, including fireworks displays, live concerts, and street parties, take place. For a great start to the year, enjoy the bustling atmosphere at Clock Tower Square or Lara Beach.

2.2 Republic Day (October 29th): Republic Day marks the founding of the Turkish Republic in 1923. Antalya celebrates this national occasion with passion and zeal. Turkish flags and decorations adorn the major streets and squares. Parades with marching bands, traditional costumes, and local dance performances may be seen. This is a fantastic chance to immerse yourself in the country's rich history while also experiencing Antalya's lively energy.

2.3 Eid al-Fitr (depending on the Islamic calendar): Ramadan, the Islamic holy month of fasting, concludes with Eid al-Fitr, also known as Ramazan Bayram. Antalya comes alive with events, wonderful traditional cuisine, and a festive atmosphere during this important holy feast. Explore the city's bazaars, where you can buy traditional gifts and eat wonderful desserts like baklava. Don't forget to express warm "Eid Mubarak" welcomes to locals you encounter during this time.

2.4 Kurban Bayram (dates vary according to the Islamic calendar): Another prominent Islamic festival observed in Antalya is Kurban Bayram, also known as Eid al-Adha. It honors Ibrahim's (Abraham's) willingness to sacrifice his son as an act of devotion to God. Families assemble to slaughter an animal and distribute the meat to relatives, friends, and those in need. During this festival, the city is filled with a spirit of kindness and togetherness.

Considerations for Action: 3.1 Transportation and Accommodation: It is important to organize your transportation and accommodations ahead of time during public holidays. During these times, Antalya might see an influx of guests, so book your reservations early to obtain the finest alternatives.

3.2 Local Customs and Politeness: When visiting Antalya during public holidays, it is essential to observe local customs and politeness. When visiting holy places, dress modestly and keep cultural sensitivity in mind. Locals would appreciate it if you greet them with traditional expressions like "Merhaba" (Hello) and "Teşekkür ederim" (Thank you).

Finally, visiting Antalya on public holidays is an excellent chance to immerse yourself in the city's culture, customs, and festive mood. Every public holiday in Antalya is different, from New Year's Day to Republic Day, including religious festivals like Eid al-Fitr and Kurban Bayram. You'll make treasured memories and get a greater

Bruce Terry

knowledge of Antalya's rich legacy by becoming acquainted with the holiday calendar and embracing local traditions. Plan your visit accordingly, and prepare to join the warm-hearted people of Antalya in celebrating these wonderful holidays.

ELECTRIC PLUG

When planning a vacation to Antalya, Turkey, it's essential to have a solid grasp of the local electrical infrastructure to guarantee a trouble-free stay. This thorough travel guide will offer you complete information on Antalya's electric plugs, including plug types, voltage, and charging advice. By being acquainted with the electrical standards, you may guarantee that your electronic equipment remains charged during your vacation to this lovely seaside city.

Plug Types in Antalya: In Turkey, including Antalya, power plugs and sockets of type F and type C are utilized. Type F plugs feature two circular pins with grounding clips, while type C plugs do not have grounding clips. These plug types are compliant with European and a variety of other international standards. To guarantee compatibility with your electrical gadgets, pack a universal adapter or the proper plug adaptor.

Voltage and frequency: Antalya's standard voltage is 230 volts, with a frequency of 50 hertz. Before connecting to your gadgets, be sure to verify the voltage requirements. Most current electronic gadgets, such as computers, cellphones, and cameras, can operate in a broad voltage range (usually 100-240 volts) with no problems. However, if you have older or specialized gadgets that work on a different voltage, you may need to utilize a voltage converter to save your equipment from being damaged.

Charging Your Gadgets: In order to charge your electronic gadgets in Antalya, you must first locate a power source that is compatible with your plug type. Many hotels, guesthouses, and lodgings have universal outlets that accept both type F and type C plugs. However, it is usually a good idea to check with your lodging ahead of time to verify that they have the necessary outlets or to pack a universal adaptor to be prepared for any circumstance.

If you're visiting Antalya, you may also find power outlets at airports, cafés, shopping malls, and other public places. Some of these sites may feature USB charging ports, allowing you to charge your gadgets without using a plug adaptor.

Considerations for Safety: When utilizing electric plugs in Antalya, it is essential to emphasize safety. Here are a few precautions to take:

Consider employing surge protectors to protect your electronic gadgets from power surges or voltage changes, which may occur on occasion.

Before connecting to your device, check the power outlets for any evidence of damage or lose connections. If you find any problems, avoid using them and notify the proper officials.

Unplug your gadgets when they are fully charged or not in use to save energy and avoid the risk of electrical accidents.

Conclusion: Understanding Antalya's electrical system and plug kinds can assist guarantee a pleasant and pleasurable vacation. You can charge your electrical gadgets easily by carrying the appropriate plug adapters, understanding the voltage requirements, and following safety standards. Remember to check with your lodging for the availability of appropriate outlets and to look into public locations that provide charging choices. With this information, you may remain connected, record great experiences, and easily traverse Antalya.

CURRENCY

The Turkish Lira (TRY) is the official currency of Turkey, which includes Antalya. The Turkish Lira is represented by the symbol "and is divisible into units known as kuruş, which are seldom used in practice.

Currency conversion rates vary on a daily basis, therefore it's essential to verify the prices before your travel. Current exchange rates may be found online at numerous financial websites or by visiting currency exchange offices.

Currencies Exchange Options:

a. Banks: Banks offer a trustworthy and safe way to exchange currencies. They are usually open throughout the week and provide reasonable exchange rates. When visiting a bank for money exchange, carry your passport with you.

b. *Exchange Offices:* Throughout Antalya, there are numerous exchange offices, also known as "döviz bürosu" in Turkish. These institutions often provide somewhat better rates than banks and are typically open for extended hours, including weekends. It is, nevertheless, essential to confirm that the exchange office is accredited and recognized.

c. *ATMs:* There are several ATMs in Antalya that enable you to withdraw Turkish Lira straight from your bank account. Keep in mind that your bank may impose foreign transaction costs, so check with your bank to see if there are any extra expenses.

Credit and Debit Cards:

Credit and debit cards are frequently accepted in Antalya's hotels, restaurants, and major retail outlets. The most generally accepted credit cards are Visa and Mastercard, followed by American Express and Diners Club. However, carrying some cash is recommended, particularly for smaller businesses or when traveling to rural regions where card acceptance may be restricted.

Currency Tips & Etiquette:

a. *Small Denominations:* Small denomination notes are recommended since smaller restaurants and taxi drivers may not always have enough change for bigger bills.

b. *Tipping:* Tipping is expected in Antalya. In restaurants, a tip of roughly 10% of the entire cost is customary. However, it is always a good idea to double-check the statement to see whether a service fee has already been included.

c. *Bargaining:* Bargaining is prevalent in local marketplaces, particularly for souvenirs. However, it is less common in bigger businesses or malls.

d. *Counterfeit cash*: As with any tourist site, counterfeit cash must be avoided. To reduce danger, it is best to exchange money at trustworthy companies.

Conclusion: Understanding the money in Antalya is vital for a stress-free vacation experience. Familiarize yourself with the Turkish Lira, exchange rates, and currency conversion possibilities. Remember to bring a variety of cash and credit cards, and be aware of currency etiquette and advice. By following these tips, you will

Bruce Terry

be able to comfortably negotiate the financial sides of your vacation while still enjoying Antalya's beauty and cultural wealth.

LANGUAGE

The official language of Turkey is Turkish, and this is the primary language spoken in Antalya. Turkish belongs to the Turkic language family and is closely related to other Turkic languages such as Azerbaijani and Uzbek. While English is widely spoken in major tourist areas and hotels, having some basic knowledge of Turkish will undoubtedly enrich your interactions with locals and help you navigate everyday situations.

Here are some essential Turkish phrases and expressions to familiarize yourself with before your trip:

Merhaba (Mehr-hah-bah) - Hello

Teşekkür ederim (Teh-shehk-kur ed-er-im) - Thank you

Evet (Eh-vet) - Yes

Hayır (Hah-yur) - No

Lütfen (Loot-fen) - Please

Benim adım [name] (Beh-nim ah-dum [name]) - My name is [name]

Ne yapıyorsunuz? (Neh yah-puh-yor-soon-ooz?) - What are you doing?

Nerede? (Neh-reh-deh?) - Where is it?

Yardım edebilir misiniz? (Yar-duhm ed-eh-beel-eer mee-see-neez?) - Can you help me?

Sağol (Sah-ol) - Thanks

When conversing with locals, it's helpful to have a few phrases related to common situations. Here are some examples:

Restoran önerebilir misiniz? (Res-toh-rahn uh-neh-reh-beel-eer mee-see-neez?) - Can you recommend a restaurant?

Bira lütfen (Bee-rah loot-fen) - Beer, please

İngilizce konuşuyor musunuz? (Een-gi-leez-jeh koh-noh-shoo-yor moos-ooz?) - Do you speak English?

Fiyatı ne kadar? (Fee-yah-tuh neh kah-dar?) - How much does it cost?

Hangi otobüs Antalya'ya gider? (Hang-ee oh-toh-boos An-tah-lyah-yah gee-der?) - Which bus goes to Antalya?

In addition to these phrases, it's useful to know basic numbers and directions. Here are a few examples:

Bir (Beer) - One

İki (Ee-kee) - Two

Üç (Ooch) - Three

Sağ (Sah) - Right

Sol (Sohl) - Left

Doğru (Doh-roo) - Straight

To further immerse yourself in the local culture and connect with the people of Antalya, consider learning a few additional phrases and customs:

Günaydın (Goo-nahy-dun) - Good morning

İyi akşamlar (Ee-yee ak-shahm-lar) - Good evening

Hoş geldiniz (Hosh gel-dee-neez) - Welcome

Nasılsınız? (Nah-suhl-suhn-uhz?) - How are you?

Türk kahvesi (Turk kah-veh-see) - Turkish coffee

Pazarlık yapabilir miyim? (Pah-zar-lik yah-pee-beel-eer mee-yim?) - Can I bargain?

While having a basic understanding of the Turkish language will undoubtedly enhance your travel experience in Antalya, don't worry if you encounter language barriers. Turkish people are generally warm, friendly, and welcoming, and they will often go out of their way to assist you, even if you don't speak their language fluently.

If you find it challenging to communicate verbally, consider using gestures, pointing at maps, or utilizing translation apps on your smartphone. Most locals will appreciate your effort to connect and will happily assist you in any way they can.

In conclusion, while English is widely spoken in Antalya's tourist areas, learning some basic Turkish phrases will undoubtedly enrich your travel experience. It will help you connect with locals, navigate everyday situations, and immerse yourself in the local culture. By making an effort to learn a few key phrases and customs, you'll be able to create memorable interactions and make the most of your time in this beautiful coastal city.

VISA REQUIREMENT

Visa Exemption: Turkey has introduced a visa waiver scheme for people from a number of countries. If you have a passport from one of these countries, you may visit Turkey, including Antalya, without a visa or with a visa obtained on arrival, depending on the length of your stay. The visa exemption only applies to stays for tourism or business. The nations listed below are eligible for visa exemption (subject to certain requirements and limitations):

Member states of the European Union

The United States

Canada

Australia

Bruce Terry

The country of New Zealand

The United Kingdom

Japan

Korea, South

Malaysia

Singapore

Brazil

Argentina

Chile

Visa on Arrival: If your country is not on the visa waiver list, you may still receive a visa on arrival at Antalya Airport or any other port of entry in Turkey. The visa on arrival permits you to remain in Turkey for up to 90 days within a 180-day period, including Antalya. However, it is always advisable to check with the Turkish embassy or consulate in your own country before going to guarantee the most up-to-date visa restrictions.

E-Visa: Travelers from qualified countries may also apply for an e-Visa online prior to their journey to Antalya. The e-Visa is a quick and easy method to get a visa without having to visit an embassy or consulate. The online application procedure is simple, and the visa is generally obtained within a few days. The e-Visa allows for a stay of up to 90 days within a period of 180 days and is eligible for tourism, business, or medical treatment.

Documents Required for Visa Application:

You will normally need the following papers to apply for a visa to visit Antalya:

Valid passport: Your passport should be valid for at least six months beyond your scheduled departure date.

Visa application form: This may be received from your country's Turkish embassy or consulate or filled out online for an e-Visa.

Passport-sized photographs: Two current, color passport-sized photos are usually needed.

Flight tickets, hotel bookings, or a vacation itinerary may all be used as proof of travel preparations.

Sufficient funds: You may be required to provide evidence that you have enough money to support your stay in Antalya.

Supporting papers: Depending on the purpose of your visit, additional documents such as a letter of invitation, evidence of employment, or a bank statement may be necessary.

Bruce Terry

Important Factors to Consider:

Visa requirements are subject to change, so check the most recent restrictions before arranging your trip.

Overstaying your visa might result in penalties, deportation, or future travel restrictions, so be sure you stick to the time limit.

If you want to work, study, or participate in any other activity in Antalya, you must apply for the necessary visa or permission.

It is recommended that you get travel insurance that covers medical expenditures while in Antalya.

To guarantee a smooth and comfortable journey, acquaint yourself with the visa requirements before coming to Antalya. You may be qualified for a visa exemption, visa on arrival, or an e-Visa depending on your nationality. Before applying for a visa or coming to Antalya, be sure you have all of the essential paperwork and satisfy the criteria. By being well-prepared, you will be able to completely immerse yourself in the beauty and culture of Antalya without having to worry about visa issues.

DIETARY RESTRICTIONS AND EATING

a. *Turkish food:* Turkish food is recognized for its rich taste and numerous vegetarian alternatives. Traditional vegetarian-friendly meze foods include hummus, filled grape leaves (dolma), and eggplant-based dishes (such as imam bayildi). Throughout Antalya, you can also discover a range of vegetable-based soups, salads, and freshly baked bread.

b. *Vegetarian and Vegan Restaurants:* Antalya has a number of vegetarian and vegan restaurants that cater to individuals who follow plant-based diets. Govinda's Vegan Restaurant, Kaleici Vegan Restaurant, and Vegetarian Restaurant 7 Mehmet are also popular choices.

Gluten-Free Diets:

a. *Celiac-Friendly Options:* Antalya's culinary scene is sensitive to the demands of gluten-free dieters. Numerous eateries provide selections that are gluten-free, and some even have gluten-free menus. With its focus on fresh seafood, grilled meats, and vegetable dishes, Mediterranean cuisine often includes gluten-free alternatives. To guarantee a comfortable eating experience, it is nevertheless recommended that you mention your dietary needs to the restaurant personnel.

b. *Gluten-Free Bakeries:* Gluten sensitivity or celiac disease sufferers can discover a variety of gluten-free bakeries in Antalya. These businesses sell bread, pastries, and sweets produced using alternative flour such as rice flour, maize flour, or chickpea flour.

Halal Food:

a. *Halal Certification:* The majority of restaurants and food enterprises in Antalya are Halal-certified, giving Muslim visitors peace of mind. Kebabs, grilled meats, pilaf, and Turkish delight are all Halal alternatives in traditional Turkish cuisine.

b. *Street Food:* Any tourist should taste Antalya's street food scene. Street booths selling Turkish favorites such as simit (sesame-coated bread rings), roasted chestnuts, and grilled corn on the cob should be avoided. These Halal street food alternatives provide a true experience of local culture.

Allergies and Special Dietary Needs:

a. *Communication with Restaurant employees:* It is important to communicate explicitly with restaurant employees if you have special allergies or dietary restrictions. While many restaurants have English-speaking employees, carrying a translated note outlining your dietary restrictions might assist to avoid misunderstanding.

b. *foreign food:* Antalya is a cosmopolitan city with a diverse selection of foreign food. Restaurants providing Asian, Italian, Mexican, and other ethnic cuisines may provide additional alternatives for those with particular dietary requirements.

Bruce Terry

Conclusion: Antalya is an excellent location for visitors with dietary restrictions, with a wide range of alternatives to accommodate a variety of tastes. You may enjoy the bright tastes of Turkish cuisine while following your dietary preferences, with selections ranging from vegetarian and vegan meals to gluten-free alternatives and Halal options. You may have a great and fulfilling eating experience in Antalya by stating your demands clearly and enjoying the various culinary scene.

CYBER CAFES

Availability and Services: Cyber cafés are reasonably simple to locate in Antalya, especially in the city center and prominent tourist locations. These businesses serve both residents and visitors, providing a variety of services geared to improve your digital connection. Cyber cafés offer the following services:

Internet Access: Cyber cafés provide high-speed internet connections, allowing for speedy and dependable access to the online world. These places provide a hassle-free internet experience, whether you need to check emails, perform research, or just surf the web.

Computer Rentals: If you don't have your own laptop or tablet, you may rent one from a cyber café. These rentals are often pre-installed with software and key programs, enabling guests to conduct duties or enjoy online amusement.

Bruce Terry

Printing and Scanning: Some internet cafés provide printing and scanning services, which may be useful for printing travel papers, boarding passes, or tickets. Check availability and price with the respective café.

Gaming Facilities: For gamers, several Antalya cyber cafés provide specialized gaming zones outfitted with powerful gaming PCs and a diverse variety of popular games. This is a wonderful alternative for gamers who want to participate in multiplayer fights or test out the newest releases while on the road.

Locations: Cyber cafés may be found all across Antalya, with a concentration in the city center and tourist districts. Here are a few noteworthy sites where reputable cyber cafés may be found:

Kaleiçi: Antalya's ancient city center, Kaleiçi, is a bustling bustle of activity and a fantastic spot to discover internet cafés. This lovely neighborhood's tiny alleyways conceal a plethora of shops that provide internet connection and computer rentals.

Lara Beach: Known for its beautiful coastline and luxurious resorts, Lara Beach also has a number of internet cafés. These facilities cater to vacationers' requirements by giving easy access to digital services while relaxing on the beach.

Konyaalt: Konyaalt, another famous beach neighborhood in Antalya, has a variety of internet cafés along the shore. Visitors may cool down in the pool before heading to a neighboring café to catch up on work or connect with friends and family.

Retail Malls: Many Antalya retail malls, including TerraCity, Mall of Antalya, and Deepo Outlet Center, provide internet cafés on their grounds. These cafés are excellent for a brief digital break while shopping.

Tips for a Smooth Experience:

Consider the following suggestions to guarantee a smooth experience at Antalya's cyber cafés:

Check Operating Hours: Confirm the hours of operation of the cyber café you want to visit, since they may differ. Some businesses stay open late, giving an alternative for tourists who want to work or browse during calmer hours.

Check Pricing: Prices for cyber cafés may vary based on criteria such as location, services supplied, and length of use. To minimize surprises, it's a good idea to enquire about the price structure ahead of time.

Personal Data Security: Use care while accessing personal accounts or sensitive information, just as you would with any public internet connection. For further protection, avoid keeping login passwords on public computers and consider utilizing a VPN.

Bruce Terry

Respect other customers by keeping noise levels to a minimum, sticking to specified gaming areas, and being aware of your surroundings. It is critical to make the Internet café a pleasant place for everyone.

Conclusion: As you go to Antalya, you can be certain that you will be able to retain your digital connection with ease. Cyber cafés in the city provide handy services such as high-speed internet access, computer rentals, and more. Whether you need to catch up on work, interact with loved ones, or just relax online, these venues offer a pleasant and dependable area for all your digital requirements. Stay connected and make the most of your Antalya experience by visiting one of the city's internet cafés.

LOCAL TIME

It is essential to remember a local time while arranging a vacation to Antalya, Turkey, to ensure a seamless and pleasurable visit. Understanding the local time zone, daylight savings time, and how it may affect your schedule will allow you to make the most of your vacation to this lovely seaside city. We will give you extensive information about Antalya's local time and all you need to know to prevent any time-related issues in the travel guide.

1. *Time Zone:* Antalya lies in the Eastern European Time Zone (EET), which is UTC+3. This time zone is shared by many large cities, including Istanbul and Athens. It is vital to remember that

Turkey observes no daylight saving time modifications and runs on a year-round standard time.

2. *Standard Time:* Antalya adheres to standard time all year. This implies that the clocks stay unchanged and the time remains constant. Consider the time difference between Antalya and your own country or any other locations you may have visited before coming to Antalya when organizing your activities.

3. *Coordinated Universal Time (UTC):* UTC is the worldwide time standard that acts as a reference point for timekeeping all around the globe. UTC+3 is Antalya's local time, which is three hours ahead of UTC. Remember this while arranging travel, connecting flights, or organizing events.

4. *Time Difference:* Depending on your location, the time difference between Antalya and other countries or cities might vary. Determine the time difference before your journey and alter your itinerary appropriately. Here are some instances of time differences between Antalya and other cities:

Antalya, Turkey: Antalya is two hours ahead of London (UTC+3 vs. UTC+1).

Antalya, Turkey is one hour ahead of Berlin (UTC+3 vs. UTC+2).

Antalya and Moscow are both in the same time zone (UTC+3).

New York, USA: Antalya is seven hours ahead of New York City (UTC+3 vs. UTC-4).

When planning your vacation and making any required preparations, keep in mind both the time difference and the journey length.

5. *Timekeeping:* There are many ways to keep track of local time in Antalya:

Watches and Clocks: Make sure your wristwatch or other timekeeping device is set to Antalya time (UTC+3). Clocks at hotels, public spaces, and transit hubs may also be relied on.

When you arrive in Antalya, most mobile phones will automatically adapt to the local time zone. However, it's a good idea to double-check that your device is set to the right time zone and, if required, manually update it.

Online Time Tools: Online time tools and websites can tell you what time it is in Antalya right now. To assure accuracy, utilize websites such as timeanddate.com or worldclock.com.

Local Authorities: If you have any special time-related questions or need exact information, you may contact local authorities, such as tourist offices or hotels, who will be able to assist you properly.

Bruce Terry

6. *Itinerary Effects:* Knowing the local time in Antalya is essential for efficiently organizing your itinerary. To prevent any time-related issues, keep the following items in mind:

Flight Arrivals and Departures: Double-check the departure and arrival timings when booking your flights, taking into consideration the time difference between Antalya and your departure/arrival city. This can help you avoid missing your flight or being delayed indefinitely.

Sightseeing and Activities: Plan your sightseeing and activities with local time in mind. Make sure to allow enough time for each attraction, as well as any time necessary for transportation or tickets.

Opening Hours: Many tourist sites, museums, stores, and restaurants in Antalya have set hours of operation. Confirm the hours of operation for the locations you want to visit and prepare appropriately.

Public Transportation: Be informed of the timetables for public transportation, such as bus or tram services, to minimize inconvenience or lengthy wait periods. Consider how long it will take to get to your location and plan your route appropriately.

By being aware of the local time in Antalya, you may assure a well-organized and pleasurable journey free of time-related complications.

Bruce Terry

Conclusion: Understanding local time in Antalya is critical for good trip planning and a smooth travel experience. Antalya is on Eastern European Time (UTC+3) all year, with no daylight saving time modifications. You may make the most of your time in Antalya by considering the time difference between your home country and other places, adapting your itinerary appropriately, and remaining informed of local timekeeping systems. Have a fantastic time in Antalya, and may your experiences be full of beautiful memories!

Bruce Terry

Bruce Terry

CHAPTER 2

BEST TIME TO VISIT ANTALYA

Summer Season (June to August): From June through August, temperatures in Antalya range from 77 to 95 degrees Fahrenheit and are marked by long, hot days with little chance of rain. This time of year is perfect for beachgoers and sunbathers who want to enjoy water sports, swimming, and sunbathing. The Mediterranean Sea's mild waters make it ideal for aquatic sports such as snorkeling and scuba diving. However, keep in mind that the summer months are also the main tourist season in Antalya, which means more people and higher rates. This is the time to come if you want a lively environment with a buzzing nightlife and want to fully feel the city's vivid energy.

Spring (April to May) and Autumn (September to October) seasons:

Antalya's transitional seasons, spring and fall, are regarded as the ideal times to come for people who like milder weather and fewer tourists. The weather is normally nice throughout these months, with temperatures ranging from 15 to 25 degrees Celsius (59 to 77 degrees Fahrenheit). Spring gives beautiful green landscapes and blossoming flowers, and fall brings perfect water temps for swimming. These seasons also provide an excellent opportunity to see Antalya's historical sights and natural marvels, such as the ancient city of Aspendos, the Düden Waterfalls, and the magnificent Saklikent Gorge, without the blazing heat and crowds.

Winter Season (November to March): Antalya has moderate winters compared to the rest of Turkey, making it an ideal location for winter tourists looking for a break from the cold. While temperatures may fluctuate from 10 to 18 degrees Celsius (50 to 64 degrees Fahrenheit) throughout this time, it is worth mentioning that the city does experience rainfall, especially in December and January. Winter in Antalya, despite the odd rain, is typically moderate and provides a calmer ambiance, making it a good season for budget visitors and those wanting a more relaxing holiday. Furthermore, visiting Antalya during the winter season enables you to take advantage of reduced hotel rates and enjoy the city's attractions with fewer people.

In general, the ideal time to visit Antalya is determined by personal interests and the sort of experience desired. Summer is ideal if you appreciate bright beach scenes, and bustling nightlife, and don't mind heavier people. The spring and fall seasons are great for individuals who like warmer weather, fewer crowds and wish to comfortably enjoy historical buildings and natural marvels. Winter, on the other hand, provides a more tranquil and cost-effective experience.

Bruce Terry

Whatever time of year you visit Antalya, it is important to carry suitable clothes, and sunscreen, and remain hydrated. Before arranging your journey, you should also check the local weather forecast and any travel warnings.

MONEY SAVING TIPS

Visit during the shoulder season: Traveling during the shoulder season (spring or fall) rather than the high summer months might greatly reduce your costs. Not only will you discover more reasonable lodging, but there will also be fewer people, making it simpler to experience famous sights at your leisure.

Use public transportation: Antalya has a well-developed public transit system, including buses and trams, which are both handy and cost-effective. Purchase an Antalya Kart, a reloadable card, to enjoy reduced costs while exploring the city and visiting important sites. It's a more affordable option than cabs or rented automobiles.

Explore Antalya's free attractions: Antalya has a number of free attractions that enable you to immerse yourself in its rich history and natural beauty without paying a thing. The Old Town (Kaleiçi), with its tiny alleyways and well-preserved Ottoman buildings, should not be missed. You may also go to the city's wonderful parks, such as Atatürk Park and Karaaliolu Park, which provide great views of the Mediterranean.

Bruce Terry

Eat at local restaurants: To enjoy traditional Turkish food while saving money, choose local restaurants and cafes over tourist traps. These establishments often provide wonderful classic foods at relatively reasonable costs. For a fast and inexpensive supper, consider street cuisine like gözleme (savory stuffed flatbread) and döner kebab.

Market bargains: Antalya's markets, including the Old Bazaar (Kaleiçi arş) and the Saturday Market, are excellent locations to buy souvenirs, spices, and textiles. To obtain the greatest bargains, remember to negotiate with the sellers. Bargaining is widespread in Turkey, and you can often negotiate a cheaper price, particularly if you purchase in bulk or pay in cash.

Stay in affordable accommodations: While Antalya has luxury resorts and high-end hotels, there are also many budget-friendly choices. Consider sleeping in guesthouses, hostels, or low-cost hotels, especially outside of the city center, where costs are often cheaper. To further lower your lodging prices, look for bargains and discounts online.

Pack sunscreen and other necessities: Antalya has a Mediterranean climate, which means it may become fairly hot and sunny throughout the summer. Pack your own sunscreen, sunglasses, and other necessities to avoid paying exorbitant costs at tourist stores.

Bruce Terry

Furthermore, carrying a refillable water bottle can keep you hydrated while saving you money on bottled water.

Plan day excursions on your own: While guided tours might be convenient, they are generally more expensive. To save money, consider arranging your day excursions on your own. Avoid the extra fees of planned excursions by using public transit or renting a vehicle to explore local sights like the ancient ruins of the Side or the picturesque Düden Waterfalls at your own leisure.

Investigate attraction passes: whether you want to visit many ticketed attractions, see whether there are any attraction passes that give lower admission prices. These permits often give discounted entrance to major locations, helping you to save money while discovering Antalya's rich cultural and historical legacy.

Avoid needless spending: Finally, keep an eye out for unnecessary expenses that may rapidly mount up. Avoid eating at tourist trap restaurants near major tourist sites, where costs are often exaggerated. Instead, bring food or a picnic to enjoy in attractive locations. Additionally, to prevent high roaming expenses, try utilizing free applications for navigation and communication.

Finally, by following these money-saving strategies, you may have a fantastic day touring Antalya without breaking the bank. There are many ways to enjoy everything that Antalya has to offer while keeping your pocketbook happy, from picking the best time to come

Bruce Terry

and using public transit to finding out budget-friendly lodgings and visiting free attractions.

CHAPTER 3

GETTING AROUND ANTALYA

It is very simple and convenient to get to Antalya, Turkey's lovely beach city. Whether you're a tourist or a native, Antalya has a number of transit choices for seeing its sights, beaches, and colorful districts. Here's a comprehensive guide on getting about Antalya:

Antalya has a significant public transit system that includes buses, trams, and minibusses (dolmuş). Buses are the most frequent means of public transit in the city and its surroundings, spanning the whole city and its surroundings. They are reasonably priced and offer a handy method to get about Antalya.

Trams are another common mode of transportation in the city center. The AntRay tramline links significant sites such as Kaleici (Old Town), the bus station (Otogar), and the Antalya Museum. Trams are an efficient, clean, and pleasant mode of transportation inside the city.

Dolmuş, or shared minibusses, are widespread in Antalya. They run on predetermined routes and are an inexpensive choice for traveling small distances or visiting surrounding communities. Dolmuş may be summoned at specified stops or by waving from the side of the road.

Bruce Terry

Taxis: Taxis may be readily called from the street or obtained at authorized taxi stops around Antalya. They are a good choice for a more convenient and direct means of transportation, particularly when traveling short distances or with baggage. However, before beginning the trip, be sure the taxi driver utilizes the meter or agrees on a fee.

Renting a vehicle: Renting a vehicle in Antalya is a popular option for those who want more freedom and independence. In the city, there are various automobile rental firms, including worldwide brands. You may explore Antalya and its surroundings at your own leisure if you rent a vehicle. However, bear in mind that traffic may be high, particularly during busy tourist seasons, and parking in certain places may be restricted.

Bicycles and scooters: Antalya encourages cycling and has a bicycle-sharing system known as AntBis. You may hire a bicycle at any of the city's stations and return it to any other station. Cycling is an environmentally benign mode of transportation, particularly for shorter distances or touring parks and seaside routes.

In certain regions, electric scooters, such as those provided by popular services such as Lime or Bird, are also available. These scooters, which can be leased using smartphone applications, are a fun and convenient way to go short distances.

Bruce Terry

Walking: The finest way to see Antalya's city center, especially the old Kaleiçi area, is on foot. You may completely immerse yourself in the city's charm, small alleyways, and historic buildings by walking. The majority of significant sites, restaurants, and stores are within walking distance, making it a nice and relaxed way to explore Antalya.

Boat tours: Due to Antalya's coastline position, there are several chances for boat tours and cruises. Explore the beautiful Mediterranean coastline, visit surrounding islands, or take a relaxing boat along the turquoise seas. Boat tours are a popular method to see the natural beauty of the area and may be booked via tour companies or directly at the dock.

Excursions & Tours: Antalya is a gateway to a plethora of intriguing sites and monuments. Numerous travel providers provide guided tours to sites such as Perge's ancient remains, Aspendos Theater, Termessos, and the natural marvels of the Taurus Mountains. These excursions often include transportation and professional guides, enabling you to discover the region's historical and natural wonders without having to worry about getting lost.

Uber and Other Ride-Hailing Services: Antalya provides ride-hailing services such as Uber as well as local alternatives such as BiTaksi. These services make it easy and frequently inexpensive to navigate the city. You may order a trip via a smartphone app and have a driver meet you at your destination. This is a good alternative if you enjoy the convenience and familiarity of ride-hailing services.

Local Ferries: Local ferries are a fantastic way to visit the coastal regions around Antalya. You may take a boat to surrounding towns like Kemer, Kaş, and Kekova. These cities are well-known for their beautiful beaches, historical buildings, and pleasant Mediterranean atmosphere. Local ferries provide a picturesque and pleasant way to explore the Turkish Riviera.

Horse Carriages: Horse-drawn carriages (fayton) provide brief excursions through the old quarter in the Kaleiçi district. A horse carriage ride, although not a practical mode of transportation, may be a fascinating and nostalgic experience that allows you to absorb the ambiance of the old town.

To summarize, moving about Antalya is a simple and fun experience, with several transportation alternatives accessible. Antalya has something for everyone, whether you like public transit, taxis, renting a vehicle, cycling, strolling, or discovering the area via boat cruises and planned tours. Choose the means of transportation that best matches your requirements and interests, and prepare to see the city's rich history, breathtaking coastline, and dynamic culture.

HOW TO GET FROM ANTALYA AIRPORT TO CITY CENTER

It is pretty simple and convenient to go from Antalya Airport to the city core. Antalya Airport (officially Antalya International Airport) is the primary airport servicing Antalya, Turkey's most popular tourist destination. Here's a step-by-step guide on getting from Antalya Airport to the city center:

Taxis are accessible at Antalya Airport and are a simple way to travel to the city core. Taxi stands are located outside the arrival hall as you depart the airport. Taxis are typically yellow and equipped with meters. However, it's always a good idea to double-check the fee and make sure the meter is turned on throughout the journey. The trip from the airport to the city center takes around 20-30 minutes, depending on traffic.

Shuttle Bus: A shuttle bus from Antalya Airport to the city center is another alternative. Several shuttle services operate from the airport, transporting passengers to different Antalya locations. The shuttle buses are normally situated outside the terminal building, and signage identifying their departure spots is plainly visible. The benefit of riding a shuttle bus over a cab is that it is less expensive. However, bear in mind that shuttle buses normally run on a set schedule, so double-check the schedule ahead of time.

Public Bus: Public buses link Antalya Airport to the city core. The bus station is situated just outside the international terminal. You may take the 600 bus that runs between the airport and the city center. The buses are spacious and have air conditioning. The trip to the city center takes between 30 and 40 minutes, depending on traffic. Some buses may not take credit cards, so bring some Turkish Lira (TRY) in cash.

Private transport: If you want a more customized and hassle-free experience, private transport from Antalya Airport to the city center may be arranged. In Antalya, several private transfer companies operate, providing a variety of alternatives such as cars, minivans, and even luxury vehicles. Transfers may be booked online or via your hotel. A private transfer assures that you will be met at the airport by a driver and will not have to worry about finding transportation upon arrival.

Renting a vehicle may be a realistic alternative if you want to explore Antalya and its environs extensively. At Antalya Airport, many automobile rental firms have offices. You may reserve a vehicle ahead of time or hire one when you arrive. Having a vehicle allows you to go at your own speed and see the different sights in and around Antalya. However, bear in mind that traffic in the city center may be busy, and parking in certain places may be difficult.

Consider your budget, travel preferences, and the quantity of baggage you're carrying before making a selection. It's also critical to verify the most recent information on transit alternatives, rates, and timetables since these might change over time. Considering these considerations will assist you in selecting the most appropriate and convenient mode of transportation from Antalya Airport to the city center, ensuring a smooth start to your vacation to Antalya.

HOW TO GET FROM ANTALYA AIRPORT TO THE NEAREST HOTELS

The journey from Antalya Airport to the closest hotels is pretty simple. Antalya Airport (IATA: AYT), commonly known as Antalya International Airport, is situated around 13 kilometers northeast of the city center. Here's a step-by-step guide on getting from the airport to neighboring hotels:

Taxis are easily accessible outside the airport terminal at authorized taxi stands. Look for the designated taxi stand and get in line. Taxis are generally yellow and equipped with a meter. Ensure that the meter is turned on throughout your ride. Taxis are an easy and handy choice, especially if you have a lot of baggage or want a direct ride to your accommodation. Make sure you have your hotel's address written down or on your phone so you can give it to the taxi driver.

Shuttle Service: Many Antalya hotels provide shuttle services to their visitors. It is best to check with your hotel ahead of time to see whether they provide airport transportation. If they do, there should be a specified meeting area at the airport where you can locate the shuttle. Because these shuttles are often shared with other guests, there may be a little wait before the vehicle leaves. The benefit of shuttle services is that they are typically inexpensive and may drop you off at your hotel.

Antalya has a well-developed public transportation system, which includes buses that go from the airport to numerous metropolitan sites. To use public transportation, go to the airport bus station, which is located directly outside the terminal building. Look for signs showing where the buses will stop. Bus numbers and routes may change, so check the information desk or the official website for the most up-to-date information. Buses are typically inexpensive, however, they may be packed, particularly during peak hours.

Rent a vehicle: If you prefer the convenience of having your own transportation, hiring a vehicle is an alternative. Several car rental companies operate booths at Antalya Airport, where you may check pricing and reserve a vehicle in advance. Once you've picked up your rental vehicle, follow the signs to the city center and use a navigation system or GPS to find your hotel. Keep in mind that driving in a foreign nation may have different rules and road conditions, so get acquainted with local driving requirements before embarking.

Private transport: Booking a private transport service is another handy alternative. Pre-arranged private transportation from Antalya Airport to hotels is available from a number of firms. You may order these services in advance online by entering your airline and hotel information. A driver will be waiting for you in the arrival hall with your name written on a sign and will help you with your bags. Private transports provide the comfort, privacy, and convenience of personalized service.

Before you finalize your vacation arrangements, consider your budget, the location of your hotel, the number of people going with you, and the quantity of baggage you have. Each choice has benefits and cons, so choose the one that best fits your tastes and requirements.

PUBLIC WIFI AVAILABILITY IN ANTALYA

Free Public WiFi Hotspots: Antalya has a plethora of free public WiFi hotspots located across the city, guaranteeing that guests have easy access to the internet. These hotspots are often found in well-known tourist destinations such as parks, beaches, city squares, and retail districts. Furthermore, many hotels, restaurants, cafés, and even public transit hubs provide their clients with free

Bruce Terry

WiFi. This extensive accessibility enables you to have a smooth internet experience while in Antalya.

Antalya Municipality WiFi: The Antalya Municipality has made major measures to improve city connectivity. They have set up a network of WiFi connection sites in public places such as parks, gardens, and cultural attractions. These access points are often referred to as "Antalya WiFi" and provide free internet access. You can enjoy consistent access while touring Antalya's colorful districts and sites by connecting to the Antalya Municipality WiFi.

Antalya Airport WiFi: When you arrive in Antalya, you may quickly connect to the internet owing to the airport's WiFi availability. The airport provides free WiFi throughout its terminals, enabling you to remain connected as soon as you arrive. Whether you need to check emails, make travel plans, or just surf the web, the airport WiFi keeps you connected from the time you step off the aircraft.

Cafes, Restaurants, and Hotels: There are several cafes, restaurants, and hotels in Antalya that provide free WiFi to their clients. From quiet coffee shops to sophisticated dining venues, you may remain connected while enjoying a meal or a cup of Turkish tea. Many Antalya hotels have free WiFi in their guest rooms and public spaces, enabling you to organize your day's activities or relax with your favorite online material.

Bruce Terry

Mobile Network Coverage: Antalya offers strong mobile network coverage in addition to public WiFi. Throughout the city, major mobile network carriers provide dependable 3G, 4G, and 5G networks. This means that even if you are outside of the WiFi range, you may still use your mobile data plan to access the internet. Check with your cell phone provider to see whether they provide international roaming, or consider getting a local SIM card for inexpensive data access during your visit.

Tips for Making the Most of Public WiFi:

When using public WiFi networks, it's best to be cautious and emphasize security. When using public WiFi, avoid inputting sensitive information or making financial activities.

For an extra degree of protection, use a virtual private network (VPN). VPNs encrypt internet traffic, shielding it from any dangers.

While using public WiFi, stay mindful of your surroundings to prevent being a target for theft or other security issues.

To avoid possible vulnerabilities, keep your devices up to speed with the newest software and security updates.

Conclusion: Antalya understands the necessity of connection for guests and provides a plethora of public WiFi alternatives across the city. Staying connected is simple, thanks to free hotspots in popular places and WiFi supplied by cafés, restaurants, hotels, and the

Antalya Municipality. Furthermore, Antalya Airport assures you that you may connect to the internet as soon as you arrive. You may make the most of your vacation to Antalya by using public WiFi and cell network coverage, remaining connected and informed during your tour.

CHAPTER 4

WHAT YOU NEED TO PACK ON A TRIP TO ANTALYA

• WHAT TO PACK FOR WINTER

Warm Clothing: Although the winters in Antalya are mild, temperatures may dip, particularly at night. To guarantee warmth and comfort, bring the following items:

a. *Thermals/Base Layers:* Bring a pair of thermal shirts and bottoms to layer beneath your usual attire for added insulation.

b. *Sweaters/Jumpers:* Keep a few lightweight sweaters or jumpers on hand for layering. For increased insulation, use fabrics such as wool or fleece.

c. *Jackets/Coats:* Bring a medium-weight jacket or coat to shield yourself from the chilly nighttime temperatures.

d. *Scarves, Hats, and Gloves:* Bring scarves, hats, and gloves to keep your extremities warm, particularly on cold nights or windy days.

Footwear: Choosing the proper footwear for winter travel is critical. While Antalya's winter isn't very cold, it's important to wear thick shoes to protect your feet from rain and wetness. Consider the following alternatives:

a. *Boots:* Bring a pair of waterproof boots or sturdy walking shoes with a strong grip to protect your feet from rain or mud when visiting outdoor regions.

b. *shoes:* Bring a pair of comfy shoes for indoor activities or walks that are not strenuous.

Layered clothing is essential for adapting to shifting temperatures and being comfortable throughout the day. Pack a range of clothing items that may be layered:

Pack multiple long-sleeved shirts that may be easily matched with sweaters or worn alone, depending on the climate.

a. *T-shirts:* Pack a couple of lightweight t-shirts to use as base layers or on their own on warmer days.

b. *Trousers/Pants:* Bring a variety of jeans, trousers, and leggings to layer beneath your coat and combine with various shirts.

Accessories: In addition to warm clothes, consider taking the following items to improve your comfort during your Antalya winter vacation:

a. *Warm socks:* Bring several pairs of warm socks to keep your feet toasty.

b. *Sunglasses:* Antalya has plenty of sunlight even in the winter. Bring some sunglasses for eye protection.

c. *Umbrella:* Although rain is less common in the winter, it's always a good idea to have a small umbrella on hand in case of an unexpected downpour.

Miscellaneous Items: To guarantee a smooth and comfortable winter journey, include the following miscellaneous items:

a. *prescriptions:* Bring any prescription prescriptions or over-the-counter medications you may need during your stay.

b. *Power Adapter:* If you are going from a country with different plug types, bring a power adapter that is compatible with Turkish outlets.

c. *Backpack or Day Bag:* Bring a lightweight backpack or day bag to carry your necessities on day trips or excursions.

Conclusion: Packing wisely for a winter vacation to Antalya guarantees that you are comfortable and get the most out of your visit. You'll be well-prepared to appreciate the beautiful beauty and cultural activities that this Turkish seaside city has to offer if you consider the moderate winter temperature and follow our complete advice. Check the local weather prediction before you go to make any required changes to your packing list.

Bruce Terry

• WHAT TO PACK FOR SPRING

Clothing:

Lightweight and breathable clothes: To remain cool throughout the day, pack lightweight and breathable clothing such as t-shirts, shorts, skirts, and dresses.

Long-sleeved shirts and trousers: It's a good idea to take a couple of long-sleeved shirts and pants for chilly nights or excursions to holy places.

Layering options: Because temperatures in Antalya may vary, bring a light jacket or cardigan for layering, particularly during chilly mornings or nights.

Swimsuits & beachwear: Antalya is well-known for its gorgeous beaches, so bring your swimsuit, cover-up, and flip-flops.

Pack comfortable walking shoes or sandals that are good for extended walks since you will most likely be touring the city and its attractions.

Accessories and necessities:

Sunglasses and hat: Pack sunglasses and a wide-brimmed hat to protect yourself from the sun's rays.

Sunscreen: Even in spring, the sun may be fierce in Antalya, so bring a high-SPF sunscreen to protect your skin.

Bruce Terry

Although spring in Antalya is normally dry, it's always a good idea to bring a small umbrella or a lightweight rain jacket in case of unexpected rains.

Tote bag or daypack: During your trips, a compact daypack or tote bag will come in useful for carrying basics such as water, sunscreen, a camera, and snacks.

Electronics and travel documents:

Passport and travel papers: Keep your passport, visa (if necessary), and any other essential travel documents in a secure and immediately accessible location.

Travel adapters: Antalya employs European standard Type C and Type F electrical outlets, therefore bring the necessary travel adapters.

Mobile phone and charger: Don't forget your mobile phone and charger, since they will be helpful for navigation, communication, and memory capture.

Toiletries and medications:

Prescription drugs: If you use any prescription prescriptions, carry enough for the length of your vacation.

Basic first-aid supplies: Pack a modest first-aid kit with bandages, painkillers, antihistamines, and any other personal prescriptions or products you may need.

Bring travel-sized amenities such as a toothbrush, toothpaste, shampoo, conditioner, and any other personal care things you may need.

Miscellaneous:

Carry a travel guidebook or maps with you to assist you explore the city and organize your activities.

While many people in Antalya understand English, having a basic language translator or phrasebook on hand might help with conversation.

Snacks and reusable water bottles: To keep hydrated and nourished throughout your adventures, bring some snacks and a reusable water bottle.

To prevent overpacking, remember to pack light and prioritize necessities. Additionally, check the Antalya weather prediction closer to your travel date to make any required changes to your packing list. You'll be well-prepared for your spring vacation to Antalya if you pack the correct apparel, accessories, and supplies.

Bruce Terry

• WHAT TO PACK FOR SUMMER

Lightweight clothes: Because Antalya has scorching summers, bring lightweight and breathable clothes. Choose natural textiles such as cotton or linen for loose-fitting shirts, tank tops, shorts, skirts, and dresses. These fabrics promote air circulation and keep you cool in hot weather. Don't forget to bring some swimsuits or trunks to enjoy the beaches.

Sun protection is essential in Antalya due to the abundance of sunlight. Pack a wide-brimmed hat or cap to keep the sun off your face. Remember to carry shades to shield your eyes from UV radiation. Also, bring sunscreen with a high SPF and apply it liberally throughout the day. Sunburns may be soothed with a travel-sized aloe vera gel.

Wear comfortable shoes: Antalya has a variety of activities, such as discovering ancient ruins, wandering along the beach, and enjoying the active nightlife. It is important to wear comfortable shoes. Pack durable walking shoes or sneakers for touring, as well as sandals or flip-flops for the beach. If you want to explore rough regions or engage in water activities, bring water shoes.

Beach necessities: Because Antalya is known for its immaculate beaches, bring beach necessities with you. Bring a beach towel, a beach bag, and a beach mat for extra comfort. Remember to bring your favorite beach book, a beach umbrella or parasol for shade, and a cooler bag to keep your beverages and food cold.

Lightweight layers: While the days in Antalya might be blisteringly hot, the nights can be refreshingly pleasant. Pack a few lightweight garments to keep you warm as the weather drops, such as a light cardigan or a thin jacket. This is particularly necessary if you want to go out at night or explore the nearby mountains.

Mosquito Repellent: Mosquitoes are common in Antalya during the summer months. Pack insect repellant to protect yourself against mosquito bites. Choose a product that contains DEET or other suggested components. Consider bringing lightweight, long-sleeved shirts and slacks to wear in the evenings.

Travel papers and Essentials: Pack any essential travel papers, such as your passport, visa (if necessary), and travel insurance information. Keep them in a safe location, such as a travel wallet or a waterproof bag. Remember to pack a universal power adaptor, since the electrical outlets in Turkey may vary from those in your native country.

Drugs and First Aid Kit: If you need prescription drugs, make sure you carry enough for the length of your trip. Pack a basic first-aid kit with items like sticky bandages, antibacterial ointment, painkillers, and any personal drugs or supplies you may need.

Bruce Terry

Bring a reusable water bottle with you to remain hydrated throughout the day. It's also a good idea to carry a travel-size umbrella or a lightweight rain jacket in case of rain in Antalya throughout the summer. Bring a daypack with you for day outings, city tours, or hiking in neighboring natural regions.

You'll be well-prepared for a summer vacation to Antalya if you bring these necessities. Remember to prepare for your own wants and tastes, and allow space in your suitcase for any mementos or goods you may buy while on vacation. Have a wonderful trip to the lovely city of Antalya!

- **WHAT TO PACK FOR AUTUMN**

Lightweight clothing: Autumn in Antalya is warm, with typical highs ranging from 20°C to 25°C (68°F to 77°F) and milder nights. Pack lightweight, breathable attire for the day, such as T-shirts, shorts, skirts, and dresses. Light sweaters or cardigans are perfect for layering on chilly nights.

Long-sleeved shirts and trousers: Pack a couple of long-sleeved shirts and pants for increased warmth as the evenings become colder. Choose soft fabrics like cotton or linen that will keep you warm without overheating.

Jackets or outerwear: Although temperatures are normally pleasant, it's a good idea to bring a light jacket or sweater with a wind-resistant layer in case of cold nights or unexpected weather changes. In case of rain, a waterproof jacket or raincoat is also important.

Footwear: For visiting Antalya's outdoor attractions, like historical monuments or hiking trails, comfortable walking shoes are a requirement. Pack closed-toe shoes for more difficult terrain and comfy sandals or flip-flops for beach trips or leisurely strolls.

Swimwear: While the fall season is not as hot as the summer, you may still choose to visit Antalya's beautiful beaches or hotel pools. Bring your best swimsuit or swim trunks for a cool plunge.

Accessories: Don't forget to carry a hat or cap to shield yourself from the sun's rays, particularly if you're going on a day trip. Sunglasses and sunscreen are also necessary for protecting your skin and eyes from UV radiation.

Evening attire: Antalya has a thriving evening culture, with several restaurants and pubs. Consider bringing a couple of dressier or smart-casual clothes for a fun night out.

Remember to include your trip papers, such as passports, IDs, and travel insurance. Bring a universal travel adaptor as well, since Turkey utilizes Europlug types C and F connections.

Prescriptions and personal care items: If you use prescription prescriptions, bring enough for the length of your vacation. Bring

Bruce Terry

personal care products such as toiletries, bug repellent, and any other necessities you may need.

A lightweight daypack or backpack is ideal for transporting your needs while touring Antalya. It's ideal for carrying water bottles, food, a camera, sunscreen, and a light jacket.

Check the weather prediction before leaving for Antalya and make any necessary changes to your packing list. Packing wisely will guarantee that you have a comfortable and happy fall trip in this lovely seaside region.

Bruce Terry

Bruce Terry

CHAPTER 5

TOP TOURIST DESTINATIONS IN ANTALYA

Kaleici (Old Town): Kaleici is Antalya's heart and soul, with its small alleyways, Ottoman-era buildings, and pleasant ambiance. Take a trip around the old city walls, see Hadrian's Gate, and explore the gorgeous marina. Kaleici also has a plethora of boutique boutiques, small cafés, and restaurants providing traditional Turkish food.

Antalya Museum: For history and cultural buffs, the Antalya Museum is a must-see. The museum exhibits an outstanding collection of ancient antiquities, including sculptures, mosaics, and ceramics. The exhibitions give an in-depth look at the region's rich archaeological legacy, making it a fascinating experience for anyone.

Aspendos: Aspendos is an old Roman city famous for its extraordinarily well-preserved amphitheater. Because of its outstanding acoustics, this spectacular edifice, erected in the second century AD, is still utilized for concerts and events today. Exploring the remains of Aspendos enables tourists to see the Roman Empire's magnificence up close.

Nature enthusiasts will be delighted by the Duden Waterfalls, which are located only a short distance from the city center. The Lower

Bruce Terry

Duden Waterfall flows right into the Mediterranean Sea, making for a breathtaking spectacle. Take a boat ride to see the falls from a new angle, or have a picnic in the neighboring park.

Konyaalti Beach: Antalya's Konyaalti Beach is a haven for sunbathers and watersports lovers. It provides the ideal atmosphere for leisure, with its crystal-clear turquoise waters, pebbled coastline, and stunning views of the Taurus Mountains. Beachfront cafés, restaurants, and water sports facilities round out the experience.

Perge: Travel a little distance outside of Antalya to see the historic city of Perge. This archaeological site has well-preserved Roman remains such as a theater, stadium, and a magnificent colonnaded street. Wander among the ruins of this once-thriving metropolis to immerse yourself in history.

Termessos: For a more off-the-beaten-path experience, go to Termessos, an ancient city situated in the Taurus Mountains. This well-preserved archaeological site provides breathtaking panoramic vistas as well as a feeling of adventure. Explore the temple, theater, and tomb remains surrounded by lovely pine trees.

Olympos: Located on the Mediterranean coast, Olympos is a hidden treasure with gorgeous beaches and a distinct bohemian vibe. The ancient city's remains, particularly the Temple of Hephaestus, give a fascinating historical aspect to the area's natural beauty. For an amazing experience, stay in one of the eco-friendly treehouse cabins.

Phaselis: The ancient Lycian city of Phaselis is notable for its well-preserved remains and scenic surroundings. It is located on a peninsula between two ports and provides a peaceful getaway from the hectic metropolis. Explore the Roman baths, theater, and aqueducts, or just relax on the lovely pine-forested beaches.

Koprulu Canyon National Park: For those looking for adventure, a visit to Koprulu Canyon National Park is a necessity. This natural paradise provides exhilarating activities such as white-water rafting down the Köprüçay River, hiking routes through breathtaking scenery, and camping in the middle of unspoiled nature.

Conclusion: The best tourist spots in Antalya provide a wide variety of activities, from visiting ancient ruins to resting on gorgeous beaches and immersing yourself in the city's colorful culture. Antalya offers something for everyone, whether you're a history buff, a nature lover, or just looking for a great holiday. Plan a trip to this Turkish Riviera treasure and be ready to be enchanted by its beauty, history, and friendly friendliness.

Bruce Terry

CHAPTER 6

BEST BEACHES IN ANTALYA

Lara Beach: Lara Beach is a renowned beach that runs over 12 kilometers along Antalya's eastern coast. This beach is ideal for families with children due to its beautiful golden sand and shallow, quiet seas. There are also a number of beach clubs, restaurants, and water sports activities to provide a fun-filled day in the sun.

Konyaalt Beach: Located near Antalya's city center, Konyaalt Beach is a popular location for both residents and visitors. The beach has a beautiful view of the Taurus Mountains, which creates a magnificent background. It's a sandy beach and clean seas are great for swimming and sunbathing. The beach has a variety of amenities such as cafés, restaurants, and water sports centers.

Phaselis Beach: is a hidden treasure located between two wooded peninsulas in Antalya's southernmost region. This quiet beach has a calm and tranquil ambiance, making it a perfect alternative for people looking for leisure. History buffs may add a cultural touch to their beach excursion by seeing the neighboring ancient remains of Phaselis.

Patara Beach: Patara Beach, located around 80 kilometers southwest of Antalya, is noted for its unspoiled natural beauty. This magnificent sandy beach, which stretches for 18 kilometers, is part of a national park, assuring its preservation. During nesting season, visitors may enjoy sunbathing, swimming, and perhaps seeing loggerhead sea turtles.

Cleopatra Beach (Alanya): Cleopatra Beach, named after the renowned queen who is said to have swum here, is located in Alanya, a picturesque seaside town near Antalya. This Blue Flag-awarded beach has beautiful sand, clear seas, and a breathtaking view of Alanya Castle. The beach has many services, and the adjacent promenade is dotted with cafés and restaurants.

Adrasan Beach: is a hidden sanctuary nestled inside a gorgeous cove surrounded by pine-clad mountains. The beach has a tranquil and peaceful atmosphere that is ideal for a pleasant escape. Swimming in the crystal-clear seas, hiking trails nearby, and excellent seafood at coastal eateries are all options for visitors.

Kaputas Beach: Tucked down at the foot of a ravine between Kaş and Kalkan, Kaputas Beach is a tiny but wonderfully picturesque beach. The beach, accessible through a set of stairs, captivates tourists with its turquoise waves and crescent-shaped expanse of golden sand. It's an excellent location for sunbathing and snorkeling.

Olympos Beach: Located near the ancient city of Olympos, Olympos Beach blends history and natural beauty. This pebble beach, surrounded by lush nature and bordered by historic city ruins, provides a one-of-a-kind beach experience. The beach is a loggerhead sea turtle nesting site, and tourists may also explore the adjacent Chimera, a natural perpetual flame.

Cirali Beach: Located between Olympos and Adrasan, Cirali Beach provides a tranquil and untouched coastal retreat. The beach has a combination of pebbles and sand, as well as bright blue seas ideal for swimming. During the nesting season, visitors may also see endangered Caretta caretta turtles. The beach is devoid of large-scale developments, resulting in a feeling of tranquillity.

Mermerli Beach: Mermerli Beach, located in the heart of Antalya's ancient town (Kaleiçi), provides a unique combination of history and coastal appeal. This little sandy beach offers views of Antalya Harbor and the majestic Hadrian's Gate. The beach offers loungers and umbrellas, enabling guests to soak up the rays while taking in the breathtaking scenery.

Conclusion: Antalya's beaches provide a wide range of possibilities for beachgoers, from noisy and crowded to isolated and calm. Whether you desire adventure, leisure, or a combination of the two, Antalya's broad array of beaches has something for everyone. Antalya delivers an exceptional beach experience in a setting of unsurpassed beauty, from the golden sands of Lara Beach to the tranquillity of Phaselis Beach and the natural beauty of Patara Beach.

Bruce Terry

BEST RESTAURANTS IN ANTALYA

Seraser Fine Dining: Seraser Fine Dining, located inside the exquisite Maxx Royal Belek Golf Resort, gets the top rank for its superb culinary mastery. This restaurant, led by famous chefs, provides a unique combination of Turkish and Mediterranean cuisines. Seraser Fine Dining is a must-visit for an outstanding dining experience, with an elegant ambiance and great service.

Piyazci Hasan: If you're looking for traditional Turkish food, Piyazci Hasan is the place to go. This beautiful restaurant, located in Antalya's old Kaleici area, specializes in traditional delicacies including piyaz (a white bean salad) and lamb kebabs. Its pleasant ambiance and genuine friendliness contribute to its allure, making it a popular neighborhood hangout.

Mehmet: 7. Mehmet is a hidden treasure in Antalya's Old Harbor district. This lovely seafood restaurant has a lovely view of the Mediterranean Sea. 7 Mehmet specializes in offering exquisite grilled fish and seafood dishes and is known for its fresh catch of the day. A memorable eating experience is created by the mix of picturesque settings and tasty cuisine.

Dede Restaurant: Dede Restaurant, located in the Kaleici area, provides an appealing environment with its charming courtyard and Ottoman-style décor. Dede Restaurant specializes in Ottoman cuisine and provides a range of meals created using ancient recipes handed down through generations. This restaurant offers a gourmet trip through Turkey's rich culinary tradition, from exquisite lamb stews to delightful desserts.

Vanilla Lounge: Vanilla Lounge, located in the fashionable Lara area, is a modern restaurant that appeals to a wide range of tastes. Sushi, spaghetti, and gourmet burgers are among the foreign cuisines on the menu. Vanilla Lounge in Antalya provides a cosmopolitan dining experience with its trendy atmosphere, live music, and comprehensive beverage menu.

Seraser Fine Dining Beach: Located on a private beach inside the Maxx Royal Belek Golf Resort, Seraser Fine Dining Beach provides a one-of-a-kind beachside dining experience. This upmarket restaurant specializes in Mediterranean and seafood cuisine, using only the freshest ingredients and experimenting with new tastes. Enjoy a romantic sunset supper while sampling the delectable flavors of the sea.

Aynal arş Restaurant: Aynal arş Restaurant is housed in a renovated Ottoman building in Kaleici and emanates old-world beauty. The restaurant is known for its traditional Turkish cuisine and offers a broad menu that includes everything from mezes (appetizers) to exquisite grilled meats. Aynal arş is a fantastic cultural and gastronomic experience thanks to its rustic ambiance and live Turkish music.

Bruce Terry

Kirmizi Restaurant: Kirmizi Restaurant is a must-visit for a delectable combination of Turkish and Mediterranean cuisine. This restaurant, located in the popular Konyaalti area, provides a modern eating experience. Creative delicacies on the menu include lamb confit with a pistachio crust and olive oil ice cream. Kirmizi Restaurant attracts discriminating food enthusiasts with its elegant décor and inventive cuisine.

Antalya Balkçs (Antalya Fisherman): Located in the lively Marina district, Antalya Balkçs (Antalya Fisherman) displays the finest of Turkish seafood cuisine. The professional cooks at the restaurant serve a variety of grilled fish, seafood mezes, and traditional Turkish appetizers. This seafood destination appeals to both seafood lovers and those looking for a stimulating dining experience, thanks to its colorful ambiance and panoramic views of the port.

Selçuk Restaurant: Located in the ancient Hadrian's Gate neighborhood, Selçuk Restaurant serves a delectable combination of Turkish and foreign cuisines. The broad cuisine caters to all tastes, with anything from succulent kebabs to pasta dishes and steaks. The picturesque courtyard setting of the restaurant, embellished with colorful lanterns, offers a pleasant and friendly ambiance.

Finally, Antalya's food scene is a veritable treasure trove of delectable tastes and dining experiences. These top 10 restaurants in Antalya will capture your senses whether you're looking for traditional Turkish cuisine, fresh seafood, or cosmopolitan delicacies. From gourmet dining to intimate local favorites, each restaurant captures the distinct spirit of Antalya's cuisine, providing you with lasting memories of great meals and genuine Turkish hospitality.

BUDGET-FRIENDLY HOTELS IN ANTALYA

Oscar Boutique Hotel: Oscar Boutique Hotel is located in Antalya's historic Kaleiçi area and provides nice and cheap accommodations. The hotel has a lovely courtyard, a kind staff, and a fantastic complimentary breakfast. Because of its central position, guests may easily visit the old town, port, and other attractions.

Elegance East Hotel: Elegance East Hotel is located within a short walk from Konyaalt Beach and provides pleasant accommodations at reasonable prices. The hotel has contemporary conveniences, a rooftop patio with breathtaking views of the sea, and a daily breakfast. Its closeness to the beach and public transit make it an excellent alternative for those on a tight budget.

Mediterra Art Hotel: Mediterra Art Hotel is nestled inside the historic walls of Kaleiçi and provides a unique combination of history and affordability. The rooms at the hotel are nicely designed, and some even include unique artwork. A lovely courtyard, a rooftop patio, and a complimentary breakfast buffet are available to guests.

Bruce Terry

Blue Sea Garden Hotel: Located only feet from the beach, Blue Sea Garden Hotel offers pleasant accommodations at an affordable price. The hotel has a tranquil garden setting, a pool, and a restaurant offering delectable Turkish cuisine. It is a good alternative for budget tourists because of its courteous personnel and accessibility to sites like Hadrian's Gate.

Atelya Art Hotel: Atelya Art Hotel, located in the center of Kaleiçi, is a delightful boutique hotel recognized for its distinctive artwork and welcoming environment. The hotel has reasonably priced and well-appointed rooms, as well as a calm garden and a rooftop terrace with panoramic views. Guests may take advantage of a complimentary breakfast as well as convenient access to historical places.

Hotel Frankfurt: Located in the Lara neighborhood, Hotel Frankfurt is a low-cost choice near Lara Beach. The hotel has nice accommodations, a swimming pool, and a restaurant that serves delectable foreign and Turkish cuisine. It is a popular option among vacationers due to its handy position near the beach and public transit.

Antalya Inn Hotel: Located in the center of Antalya, Antalya Inn Hotel provides inexpensive lodgings without sacrificing quality. The hotel has contemporary rooms, a rooftop patio with views of the city, and a restaurant offering traditional Turkish cuisine. Its strategic position enables travelers to easily explore neighboring sites.

Olbia Hotel: Located in Kaleiçi, Olbia Hotel is a family-run company that offers affordable accommodations in a nice setting. The hotel has pleasant rooms, a beautiful courtyard, and a daily breakfast. Its closeness to historic attractions and the waterfront gives it an excellent starting point for exploring Antalya.

Puding Marina Residence: Puding Marina Residence is a low-cost hotel situated near Antalya Marina. The hotel has trendy and spacious rooms, a rooftop patio with panoramic views, and free breakfast. Because of its closeness to the marina and the busy city core, it is an ideal alternative for budget-conscious guests.

Metur Hotel: Metur Hotel is located in the center of Antalya and offers reasonable lodgings within walking distance of the old town and the port. The hotel has pleasant rooms, a pool, and a restaurant that serves traditional Turkish cuisine. Its convenient location and low costs make it a popular option for budget tourists.

Conclusion: Antalya has a variety of budget-friendly hotels that appeal to guests looking for low-cost lodgings without sacrificing comfort or quality. These hotels provide excellent value for money, ranging from boutique hotels in the historic Kaleiçi area to beachfront alternatives in the picturesque Turkish Riviera. Whether you want to visit historical places, relax on magnificent beaches, or

Bruce Terry

experience active city life, these 10 Antalya cheap hotels will make your stay pleasurable and unforgettable.

BEST LUXURY HOTELS IN ANTALYA

Maxx Royal Belek Golf Resort: Located in Belek, just outside of Antalya, the Maxx Royal Belek Golf Resort is a real luxury jewel. Elegant and large accommodations, private villas, and spectacular views of the Mediterranean Sea are available at the resort. Maxx Royal Belek Golf Resort provides a memorable vacation with its own 18-hole golf course, private beach, state-of-the-art spa, and gourmet dining choices.

Rixos Premium Belek: is a luxurious all-inclusive resort known for its superb service and facilities. This hotel provides a wonderful combination of leisure and entertainment, with exquisite rooms, private villas, and direct access to a magnificent beach. The resort also has a spa, numerous swimming pools, a water park, and a variety of food choices to meet everyone's needs.

Titanic Mardan Palace: As the name implies, Titanic Mardan Palace is a palace-style hotel that provides an extraordinary experience. The beautiful architecture, sumptuous interiors, and lush grounds create a luxurious ambiance. Spacious rooms and suites, various swimming pools, a private beach, a magnificent spa, and a choice of world-class restaurants are available to guests. This hotel definitely lives up to its reputation as one of Antalya's greatest luxury hotels.

Kempinski Hotel The Dome: The Kempinski Hotel The Dome, located in Belek, is a five-star resort that emanates elegance and refinement. The hotel has nicely designed rooms and suites with breathtaking views, as well as a private beach, multiple outdoor pools, a golf course, and a spa with a variety of services. Kempinski Hotel The Dome guarantees an exceptional stay with its outstanding service and attention to detail.

Regnum Carya Golf & Spa Resort: The Regnum Carya Golf & Spa Resort is a premium hotel that caters to both golf and spa fans. The hotel, located in Belek, has large and elegant rooms, a private beach, a championship golf course, a magnificent spa, and a range of gourmet eating options. The resort's attention to detail and dedication to client pleasure place it among the best choices for luxury tourists.

Gloria Serenity Resort: is a quiet paradise surrounded by lush nature and a magnificent shoreline. The hotel has attractively furnished rooms and suites, a private beach, a spa, and a variety of leisure activities. Gloria Serenity Resort, with its calm ambiance and exceptional service, offers a quiet getaway for those looking for a luxury holiday.

Delphin Imperial Hotel: The Delphin Imperial Hotel in Antalya provides a magnificent and opulent experience. The hotel has well-appointed suites, a private beach, three swimming pools, a water park, a spa, and a variety of eating choices. Delphin Imperial Hotel is a popular option among luxury guests due to its dedicated staff and exquisite facilities.

Akra Hotel: The Akra Hotel is a modern luxury hotel in the center of Antalya. Akra Hotel provides a sophisticated and upmarket experience with its sleek design, contemporary facilities, and breathtaking views of the Mediterranean Sea. The hotel has chic rooms and suites, a rooftop pool, a spa, a variety of eating choices, and convenient access to the city's attractions. The Akra Hotel successfully combines comfort and luxury.

Susesi Luxury Resort: Susesi Luxury Resort, located near Belek, provides an amazing luxury experience. The hotel has big and nicely designed rooms, a private beach, various swimming pools, a water park, a spa, and many eating choices. Susesi Luxury Resort provides a really luxurious experience with its exceptional service and attention to detail.

Concorde De Luxe Resort: Concorde De Luxe Resort is a premium and elegant beachside hotel. Beautifully designed rooms and suites, a private beach, multiple swimming pools, a spa, and a range of eating choices are available at the hotel. Concorde De Luxe Resort is a preferred option for luxury guests seeking leisure and comfort due to its dedicated personnel and outstanding amenities.

Finally, Antalya has a variety of premium hotels that appeal to the discriminating guest. Whether you're looking for a beachside hideaway, a golfing escape, or a relaxing spa experience, these 10 top luxury hotels in Antalya will deliver a memorable and sumptuous stay, providing a genuinely unforgettable trip on the Turkish Riviera.

BEST SHOPPING MALLS IN ANTALYA

Antalya Migros Retail Mall: As one of Antalya's first contemporary retail malls, Antalya Migros Shopping Mall is a well-known landmark. It has a wide range of stores, from well-known worldwide brands to local boutiques. In addition to a wide range of retail selections, the mall has a huge food court, a theater, and a children's play area, offering a fun shopping experience for the whole family.

TerraCity Shopping Center: TerraCity Shopping Center is a prominent fashion destination. It has nearly 180 boutiques, including major fashion labels, and provides a diverse selection of apparel, accessories, and footwear. The exquisite architecture and large layout of the mall offer a pleasant and pleasurable shopping environment. It also has a multiplex theatre and a range of food alternatives to satiate your appetite.

Bruce Terry

Deepo Outlet Center: For those looking for excellent prices and discounts, Deepo Outlet Center is a shopaholic's dream. It is located near Antalya Airport and has over 90 outlet shops that provide recognized brands at reduced costs. Deepo Outlet Center features something for everyone, from fashion and athletics to home décor and gadgets. It also has leisure options such as a bowling alley and a gaming arcade.

MarkAntalya Shopping Mall: MarkAntalya Shopping Mall, located in the city center, is a dynamic and contemporary mall that mixes shopping and entertainment. It sells apparel, accessories, and gadgets from a variety of national and international brands. The open-air architecture of the mall, abundant flora, and beautiful views of the Mediterranean Sea provides a one-of-a-kind shopping experience. It also has a movie complex and a sizable food court.

Antalya Mall: Antalya Mall is one of the city's main retail malls, with a diverse range of businesses and leisure opportunities. This mall offers a wide range of preferences, from high-end fashion and cosmetics products to electronics and home décor. It's wide layout and sophisticated architecture make for a pleasant and joyful shopping experience. A big food court, a multiplex theatre, and a bowling alley are also available at Antalya Mall.

Laura Shopping Center: Laura Shopping Center, located in the attractive resort location of Kundu, is a trendy mall with a distinctive architectural style. It has an eclectic mix of foreign and local businesses that showcase the most recent fashion trends. The mall also has cafés, restaurants, and a lively rooftop terrace with panoramic views of the Mediterranean Sea, making it a great spot to relax and unwind after a day of shopping.

5M Migros Shopping Mall: Located in Antalya's Konyaalt area, 5M Migros Shopping Mall is popular with both residents and visitors. It has a diverse selection of retailers, including apparel, electronics, and home products. Cultural events and exhibits are also held in the mall, adding a touch of art and entertainment to your shopping experience. Its food court serves a range of cuisines to please every appetite.

zdilekPark Antalya: zdilekPark Antalya is a contemporary retail mall in the Muratpaşa neighborhood of Antalya. It has a wide variety of retailers, including clothing, accessories, electronics, and home design. The mall's distinctive architectural style, which incorporates natural features and green areas, produces a refreshing and welcoming atmosphere. Visitors may dine at the food court or see a movie at the multiplex theater.

Shemall Shopping Center: Shemall Shopping Center is a well-known Antalya mall that provides a complete shopping experience. It caters to every shopper's demands with a diverse range of retailers ranging from recognized fashion brands to specialty businesses. The

Bruce Terry

mall also has a large entertainment section with a movie complex and a children's play area. Furthermore, its rooftop patio provides stunning views of the city and the Mediterranean Sea.

Terracity Shopping Mall: Located in the renowned Lara neighborhood, Terracity Shopping Mall distinguishes out for its contemporary construction and fashionable environment. It features a mix of foreign and local companies in fashion, accessories, electronics, and other categories. The mall also has a theater, a bowling alley, and a range of food choices, ensuring that everyone has a good time.

Conclusion: Antalya's shopping complexes provide tourists of all tastes with a broad and dynamic retail experience. These malls provide a diverse variety of items and services, ranging from worldwide fashion brands to local shops. The city's retail malls provide something for everyone, whether you're looking for the newest fashion trends, fantastic prices, or a delicious eating experience. Explore these 10 top Antalya shopping malls for a shopper's paradise on the picturesque Turkish Riviera.

BEST MUSEUMS IN ANTALYA

Antalya Museum: Known as one of Turkey's greatest museums, the Antalya Museum has an extraordinary collection of relics from the region's ancient civilizations. The museum provides a thorough account of Antalya's history, featuring exhibits from the Hellenistic,

Roman, and Byzantine eras, with beautiful sculptures and finely designed pottery.

Kaleiçi Museum: Located in the ancient Kaleiçi area, this modest yet interesting museum shows Antalya's rich cultural legacy. Traditional clothing, folk art, and historical pictures are among the museum's holdings, offering a look into the everyday life of the locals throughout history.

Suna & nan Kraç Kaleiçi Museum: Housed in a magnificently renovated Ottoman home, the Suna & nan Kraç Kaleiçi Museum provides a unique insight into Antalya's history and customs. The museum displays a diverse collection of objects, including ancient furniture, jewelry, and traditional textiles, enabling visitors to delve into the city's cultural heritage in a pleasant environment.

Atatürk's Home Museum: Dedicated to Mustafa Kemal Atatürk, the creator of modern Turkey, this museum maintains the historical home where Atatürk lived during his travels to Antalya. Personal artifacts, pictures, and papers relating to Atatürk are shown in the museum, offering insight into his life and his major role in molding Turkey's history.

Antalya Toy Museum: A fascinating site that appeals to visitors of all ages, the Antalya Toy Museum is ideal for families and those seeking a touch of nostalgia. The museum has a large collection of toys from many ages, ranging from old dolls and model cars to traditional Turkish toys, and provides a colorful voyage through childhood memories.

Museum of Side: This archaeological museum, located in the historic city of Side, approximately an hour's drive from Antalya, is a treasure mine of items from the ancient Greek and Roman civilizations. The displays include sculptures, mosaics, and antique coins, which provide an intriguing glimpse into the history of this ancient city.

Alanya Ancient Museum: Located near Antalya in the seaside town of Alanya, the Alanya Archaeological Museum displays ancient artifacts from the surrounding region. Exhibits range from the Bronze Age to the Byzantine Era, with highlights including ancient sarcophagi, elaborate jewelry, and Roman-century sculptures.

Antalya Ethnographic Museum: Located in the ancient Yivli Minare Mosque complex, the Ethnographic Museum provides insight into the traditional lifestyle and cultural legacy of Antalyans. The museum exhibits traditional clothing, handicrafts, and daily artifacts, allowing visitors to immerse themselves in the region's cultural identity.

Mevlana Museum: While not directly in Antalya, the Mevlana Museum is worth noting since it is situated in Konya, a few hours' drive from the city. This museum, dedicated to the famed Sufi poet and philosopher Mevlana Rumi, takes visitors on a spiritual journey through Mevlana's life and teachings. The museum's displays include manuscripts, musical instruments, and Mevlevi Order items.

Antalya Atatürk Home and Museum: Another Mustafa Kemal Atatürk museum, this landmark in Antalya's center is the home where Atatürk lived during his trips to the city. Personal possessions, pictures, and historical documents are shown at the museum, affording a look into Atatürk's life and the vital role he played in building contemporary Turkey.

Finally, Antalya's museums provide an intriguing investigation of the city's rich historical and cultural legacy. Whether you're interested in ancient civilizations, traditional arts and crafts, or the biography of Mustafa Kemal Atatürk, Antalya's museums provide a wide choice of exhibitions to suit your needs. Immerse yourself in the enthralling world of Antalya's museums, and learn about the tales and artifacts that contribute to the city's distinct character.

BEST PARKS AND GARDENS IN ANTALYA

Düden Waterfalls Park: Düden Waterfalls Park is a stunning natural beauty located on the outskirts of Antalya. Upper Düden and Lower Düden are two cascading waterfalls in the park that plunge into the Mediterranean Sea. Visitors may enjoy spectacular views of the waterfalls while strolling along the park's well-maintained walkways and relaxing in covered picnic places.

Bruce Terry

Karaalioglu Park: Karaalioglu Park, located in the center of Antalya, is a quiet oasis with sweeping views of the Mediterranean Sea. The park is filled with vibrant flowerbeds, palm palms, and well-kept lawns. It also has the famous Hdrlk Tower, a historic Roman fortress. Visitors may go on leisurely walks, enjoy a picnic, or just relax in a tranquil setting.

Atatürk Park: Atatürk Park, located in the city center, is a popular recreational area for both residents and visitors. The park's main attraction is a big artificial lake on which visitors may hire paddleboats and have a leisurely ride. The park, which is lined with chairs and shaded places, provides an ideal environment for leisure and picnics.

Antalya Zoo and Nature Park: The Antalya Zoo and Nature Park, located in a large area near Konyaalti Beach, is a refuge for nature lovers. Lions, giraffes, monkeys, and reptiles are among the many animal species found in the park. In addition to the zoo, visitors may explore the botanical garden, which has a diverse array of Mediterranean plant species.

Güllük Mountain National Park: A paradise for hikers and environment enthusiasts, Güllük Mountain National Park offers a calm respite from the city. The park, which is located northwest of Antalya, has breathtaking mountain scenery, lush woods, and dazzling waterfalls. There are various hiking paths of varied difficulty levels that enable tourists to immerse themselves in the natural beauty of the area.

Karaalioglu Park Archeological Site: This archaeological site, which lies next to Karaalioglu Park, is a treasure trove of ancient ruins. Visitors may visit the ruins of the old city walls, Roman baths, and Hadrian's Gate, a beautiful gate. The park is a must-see attraction in Antalya because of its unique combination of history and natural beauty.

Aksu Dolphinarium and Botanical Garden: The Aksu Dolphinarium and Botanical Garden, located in the Aksu neighborhood, is a pleasant destination for families. The dolphinarium puts on exciting dolphin and seal performances, while the botanical garden has a diverse collection of flora, including exotic flowers and fruit trees. Within the garden, visitors may also enjoy picnic spaces and strolling routes.

Minicity: Minicity is an interactive open-air museum that features small versions of renowned places from across the globe. It is ideal for families with children. The park, which is located in Konyaalti, offers an instructive and exciting experience for tourists by enabling them to explore scaled-down copies of renowned monuments such as the Statue of Liberty and the Eiffel Tower.

Kepez Park: One of Antalya's major green areas, Kepez Park is located in the Kepez neighborhood. The park has sprawling lawns, bike trails, playgrounds, and a gorgeous lake where visitors may rent paddleboats. It's perfect for outdoor activities including running, bicycling, and family picnics.

Termessos National Park: Termessos National Park, located in the Taurus Mountains, provides a rare blend of natural beauty and historic ruins. The park is home to Termessos, an ancient settlement built on a mountain with breathtaking views of the surrounding surroundings. Visitors may enjoy the park's unique vegetation and animals while exploring well-preserved remains like temples, theaters, and necropolises.

Whether you're looking for peace & quiet, outdoor activities, or a mix of history and nature, Antalya's parks and gardens provide something for everyone. From flowing waterfalls to ancient ruins, Antalya's open areas provide a chance to interact with the region's natural and cultural history, making them must-see sites for each tourist.

BEST NIGHTCLUBS AND BARS IN ANTALYA

Club Inferno: As one of Antalya's most well-known nightclubs, Club Inferno promises a memorable evening. It draws both residents and visitors because of its contemporary décor, amazing sound system, and vibrant environment. The club has famous DJs, live music performances, and themed events, making for an unforgettable night of dancing and entertainment.

Bruce Terry

Aura Club: Aura Club, located in Antalya's popular Kaleiçi area, is noted for its unique music choices and boisterous environment. This open-air venue has a beautiful view of the bay and provides a unique atmosphere for dancing beneath the stars. Aura Club provides an amazing nightlife experience with its numerous events and skilled DJs.

Ally's Beach Bar: Ally's Beach Bar is ideal for those looking for a more casual coastal setting. This pub, located on the famed Lara Beach, has a laid-back attitude, nice sitting spaces, and spectacular sea views. While enjoying the cool wind and sandy shoreline, enjoy delicious beverages, live music, and themed parties.

Marina Bar Street: Located inside Antalya Marina, Bar Street is a thriving hive of pubs and clubs, each with its own unique personality and music style. This renowned attraction draws a broad clientele, ranging from partygoers to music fans. Marina Bar Street provides something for everyone, from fashionable cocktail bars to dancing clubs.

Club 29: Club 29 is a high-end nightclub located inside the exclusive Titanic Deluxe Golf Belek resort. It is popular among clubgoers because of its opulent atmosphere, cutting-edge sound system, and world-class DJs. Expect an eclectic mix of electronic dance music, dazzling acts, and a vibrant environment that will have you dancing till the wee hours of the morning.

Bruce Terry

Ruby Tuesday: Located in the vibrant Konyaalt sector, Ruby Tuesday is a favorite hangout for both residents and foreigners. This multi-level facility has a stylish bar, a dance floor, and a rooftop patio with city views. While sipping on unique drinks, listen to a variety of music genres ranging from popular hits to underground sounds.

Havana Club: With its Cuban-inspired concept and energetic environment, Havana Club provides a one-of-a-kind Antalya nightlife experience. This colorful bar in the trendy Lara sector includes vivid décor, Latin music, and unusual beverages. Salsa fans may even take advantage of the venue's dancing instruction.

Q Club: Located inside the luxurious Rixos Downtown Antalya resort, Q Club combines luxury and entertainment. This high-energy venue has a large dance floor, exquisite architectural architecture, and an excellent sound system. Q Club provides a wonderful night of music and dancing, whether it's with the local DJs or renowned guest acts.

Aura Rooftop Bar: Aura Rooftop Bar is a must-visit venue for people looking for stunning views and a refined ambiance. This rooftop bar in Kaleiçi's old quarter provides panoramic views of the city and the Mediterranean Sea. Sip homemade cocktails while listening to chill-out music and taking in the lovely ambiance.

Bruce Terry

Club Inferno Park: Club Inferno Park, located in the renowned Konyaalt Beach Park, is an open-air venue that merges nature with nightlife. With its beautiful surroundings, outdoor dance floor, and spectacular light displays, this club provides a one-of-a-kind experience. Dance beneath the stars to the rhythms of famous DJs, making memories that will last a lifetime.

Finally, Antalya's thriving nightlife culture provides a wealth of possibilities for partygoers and night owls. The city caters to a wide range of interests and inclinations, from high-energy nightclubs to laid-back beach bars. The 10 greatest nightclubs and bars in Antalya mentioned above guarantee fantastic evenings packed with music, entertainment, and the city's throbbing atmosphere, whether you're looking for an exciting dance floor experience or a quiet evening by the beach. So, prepare to immerse yourself in Antalya's exciting nightlife and make unforgettable experiences.

NIGHTLIFE IN ANTALYA

- **LIVE MUSIC**

Traditional Turkish Music: To really understand Antalya's local music culture, one must enter into the enthralling realm of traditional Turkish music. Traditional instruments such as the oud, kanun, and ney form a sonic tapestry. Discover the enchantment of Turkish folk music in venues such as the Antalya Culture Center and the Aspendos Amphitheatre, where traditional music events are often staged. Immerse yourself in the haunting melodies, rhythmic rhythms, and passionate voices that recount old Anatolian stories.

Antalya also caters to followers of modern music genres, with a number of venues hosting live performances by local and international performers. The following are some noteworthy places in the city to hear live music:

a. *Club Inferno:* A famous nightlife hotspot known for its explosive live music performances, Club Inferno is located in the center of Antalya. The facility showcases a broad variety of genres, from rock and pop to techno and jazz, guaranteeing that there is something for everyone. Enjoy the thrilling ambiance and skilled musicians while dancing the night away.

b. *Piano Rouge:* Piano Rouge, tucked away in the picturesque streets of Kaleiçi, Antalya's ancient town, provides a more intimate environment for live music fans. This little piano bar has great pianists and singers who play a wide range of music, including jazz, blues, and soul. Sit back, drink a glass, and allow the soft melodies to take you to another time and place.

c. *Antalya Arena:* Antalya Arena, a larger-scale arena, holds big concerts and music festivals throughout the year. International superstars and well-known Turkish performers take the stage, drawing music fans from all over the world. Check the event calendar to schedule your stay around a live performance or festival that appeals to your musical tastes.

Antalya is host to a number of music festivals and events that exhibit a wide range of genres and cultural influences. These events provide a wonderful chance to sample the local music scene while also taking in the colorful ambiance of the city.

a. *International Antalya Piano event*: Held yearly, this famous event brings together renowned pianists from all over the globe. The festival, which includes solo recitals, chamber music concerts, and seminars, is a must-see for classical music fans.

b. *Antalya International Jazz event*: Jazz fans will enjoy this vibrant event, which brings together outstanding jazz artists to play in different locations across the city. The event emphasizes the variety of the genre and features local talent with international luminaries, ranging from smooth jazz to avant-garde improvisations.

c. *Sandland Music Festival:* The Sandland Music Festival delivers a one-of-a-kind sensory experience by combining the beauty of sand sculptures with live music. Visitors may enjoy live performances by artists of many genres against the background of spectacular sand art masterpieces. This family-friendly festival appeals to both music and art fans.

Bruce Terry

Finally, Antalya's live music scene offers a plethora of options to immerse yourself in the musical charms of Turkish culture and foreign music. Antalya provides an exceptional experience for music aficionados of all sorts, whether they enjoy classic Turkish sounds, current genres, or the thrill of music festivals. So pack your luggage, be ready to be fascinated by the rhythms, and let live music lead you around this enthralling city on the Turkish Riviera.

- **ROMANTIC EVENING**

Sunset stroll through Antalya's lovely Old Town (Kaleici): Begin your romantic evening with a leisurely stroll through the gorgeous tiny alleyways of Kaleici. Explore the wonderfully preserved Ottoman-era mansions, boutique boutiques, and hidden jewels along the road. As the sun starts to set, go to the historic city walls or the Old Harbor to watch the sunset over the Mediterranean Sea.

Dinner with a View: There are various rooftop restaurants and coastal diners in Antalya that provide panoramic views of the city's coastline. Enjoy a tasty dinner while taking in the breathtaking scenery. You'll discover a broad range of eating alternatives to suit your tastes, from traditional Turkish cuisine to cosmopolitan pleasures. For a genuinely authentic experience, eat local favorites like kebabs, mezes (appetizers), and baklava (a sweet pastry).

A romantic boat sail around the shore will allow you to see Antalya's magnificent coastline from a new viewpoint. Sail along the pristine seas, through cliffs, secluded coves, and gorgeous beaches. Many cruise lines provide dining alternatives on board, enabling you to dine by candlelight while admiring the majestic splendor of the Mediterranean Sea. The relaxing sound of waves and the lovely sea wind create an intimate and unique ambiance.

Evening at Duden Waterfalls: Head out of town to Duden Waterfalls, which are around 10 kilometers from Antalya. These majestic waterfalls drop into the sea, producing a dramatic and breathtaking picture. The waterfalls are lighted as evening approaches, giving a lovely glow over the surroundings. Enjoy the tranquillity of the natural surroundings by taking a leisurely stroll along the designated routes with your loved one.

Moonlight Beach Walk: Antalya is known for its stunning beaches, and a moonlight stroll along the sandy coastlines is a romantic must-do. Find a peaceful location, throw out a blanket, and spend some time together listening to the soothing waves smashing against the coast. The moon's reflection on the lake, along with the chilly air, adds a magical touch to the environment, making it a wonderful evening for couples.

Attend a Cultural Performance: Learn about Turkish culture by attending a traditional Turkish dance or music performance. Antalya has a variety of venues where you may see enthralling events that highlight the country's rich past. These performances, which range

Bruce Terry

from whirling dervishes to folk dances, are not only amusing but also give a greater insight into Turkish traditions and customs.

Antalya, with its stunning combination of natural beauty, historical attractions, and energetic environment, sets the mood for a really romantic evening. Whether you want to stroll through the Old Town, have a candlelit dinner with a view, go on a yacht cruise, see the mesmerizing Duden Waterfalls, go for a moonlit beach walk, or see a cultural performance, Antalya has a variety of experiences to create cherished memories with your loved one. Antalya, with its enticing appeal and romantic ambiance, is surely a resort that will captivate you and leave you wanting to return.

HEALTH AND SAFETY

Travel Insurance: It is strongly advised that you purchase comprehensive travel insurance before departing for Antalya. This will cover any unanticipated medical crises, vacation cancellations, lost possessions, or other catastrophes. Check that your insurance covers medical care, repatriation, and personal responsibility.

Vaccinations & Medical Facilities: Antalya has a well-developed healthcare system, with both public and private institutions providing high-quality medical services. Carry a list of emergency contact numbers and locations of local hospitals or clinics with you. While no particular vaccines are necessary for admission into

Antalya, it is always a good idea to consult with your doctor about any suggested immunizations for Turkey.

Drugs & Prescriptions: If you need to take any prescribed drugs, make sure you have enough for the length of your stay in Antalya. It is best to keep the pills in their original packaging and bring a copy of the prescription with you. If you have any medical concerns, speak with a local physician or pharmacist who can help you acquire the required drugs or prescriptions.

Water and Food Safety: While tap water is typically acceptable for personal hygiene, bottled water is advised for drinking and brushing teeth. When eating at street food vendors or small cafes, be careful; choose freshly prepared food and avoid undercooked or unpeeled fruits and vegetables. Furthermore, ensure that the restaurant adheres to standard hygienic measures, such as clean utensils and food processing facilities.

Sun Protection: Antalya has a Mediterranean climate with long, scorching summers. Apply a broad-spectrum sunscreen with a high sun protection factor (SPF), wear a wide-brimmed hat, and wear sunglasses to protect yourself from damaging ultraviolet (UV) radiation. Seek shade during the warmest portions of the day (usually between 11 a.m. and 3 p.m.), and drink lots of water to keep hydrated.

Bruce Terry

Transit Safety: Use care and be aware of your things while using public transit in Antalya. Keep a watch on your possessions, particularly in busy locations and on buses. It is advised to utilize licensed taxis or trustworthy ride-hailing services. If you want to hire a vehicle, get acquainted with local traffic laws and drive carefully.

COVID-19 Considerations: Given the current COVID-19 pandemic, it is critical to be informed of the most recent travel recommendations and instructions published by local authorities and the World Health Organization (WHO). Wearing face masks, exercising physical distance, and periodically cleaning hands are all suggested safety precautions. To protect visitor safety, Antalya has adopted safety standards in hotels, restaurants, and tourist sites.

Emergency Preparedness: In the event of an emergency, phone 112, Turkey's universal emergency number, for quick help. For emergency circumstances, it is good to acquire a basic comprehension of popular Turkish words. Familiarize yourself with the location of your embassy or consulate in Antalya in case you need extra assistance.

Conclusion: By addressing your health and safety concerns when visiting Antalya, you can enjoy a relaxing and worry-free trip. Remember to have adequate travel insurance, bring essential medicines, observe water and food safety requirements, wear sunscreen, and remain up to date on COVID-19 practices. By following these measures, you will be able to completely appreciate the beauty and charm that Antalya has to offer.

PHARMACY AND FIRST AID

Pharmacies in Antalya: Pharmacies, also known as "Eczane" in Turkish, are extensively accessible across the region. They play an important role in the provision of pharmaceuticals, over-the-counter medications, and general health advice. Here are some important aspects to consider while looking for pharmacies in Antalya:

a. *Hours of Operation*: Most pharmacies are open from 8:30 a.m. to 7:00 p.m. on weekdays and from 9:00 a.m. to 6:00 p.m. on weekends. However, there are 24-hour pharmacies (Nöbetçi Eczane) in each district, guaranteeing that medicine is accessible at all times.

b. *Prescription medicine:* If you need prescription medicine, bring enough for the length of your trip. It is recommended that you bring your prescriptions or a note from your doctor, as this may make it easier to get essential drugs locally.

c. *Non-Prescription Medication:* Antalya pharmacies have a broad variety of non-prescription drugs, including pain relievers, antihistamines, digestive aids, and more. The pharmacist can help you choose the right drug depending on your symptoms.

d. *Language Barrier:* While many pharmacists in tourist locations speak English, it's a good idea to have a list of generic names for popular prescriptions on hand or to use translation software to aid with the conversation if language hurdles emerge.

First Aid and Medical Help: In the case of a medical emergency, it is critical to understand how to get first aid and medical help. Here's what you should know:

a. *Emergency Phone Number*: In Turkey, call 112 from any phone to contact emergency services. This number links you to an operator who will deploy emergency services such as ambulances, cops, and firemen.

b. *Hospitals and Medical institutions:* Antalya is home to a number of well-equipped hospitals and medical institutions that provide a full range of healthcare services. Antalya's well-known hospitals include Akdeniz University Hospital, Antalya Education and Research Hospital, and American Hospital Antalya. These hospitals feature bilingual personnel and provide emergency care as well as specialist medical treatments.

c. *Travel Insurance:* Travel insurance that covers medical expenditures and emergency evacuation is strongly recommended. Familiarize yourself with your policy's terms and conditions to ensure you understand the coverage and processes for obtaining medical care.

d. *First Aid Kit:* It is recommended that you bring a basic first aid kit with you while visiting Antalya. Bandages, adhesive tape, antiseptic solution, painkillers, and other personal prescriptions or supplies you may need should be included.

Conclusion: For a safe and pleasurable journey while seeing Antalya's lovely city, being aware of the available pharmacy services and knowing how to seek first aid and medical help is crucial. Antalya pharmacies provide a broad selection of prescription and non-prescription pharmaceuticals, while hospitals and medical centers provide full healthcare services. By carefully planning, including packing required prescriptions, obtaining travel insurance, and keeping a first aid kit on hand, you can assure a worry-free stay and truly appreciate Antalya's beauty and culture.

Bruce Terry

Bruce Terry

CHAPTER 7

FOOD AND DRINK

• LOCAL DRINKS

Ayran: Ayran is a popular and refreshing traditional Turkish drink found across Antalya. Ayran is a refreshing drink made with yogurt, water, and a dash of salt that is ideal for hot summer days. Its creamy texture and tangy flavor create a cooling effect, making it an ideal companion to hot foods. Ayran may be found at local restaurants, street food booths, and even supermarkets pre-packaged.

Rak: Known as Turkey's national alcoholic beverage, Rak has a distinct position in Antalya's drinking culture. Rak, often known as "lion's milk," is an anise-flavored liquor that becomes milky white when blended with water. It is typically drunk after diluting it with ice-cold water and served with a variety of mezes (appetizers). Rak sofras is the process of gently drinking Rak while participating in a vibrant discussion with friends. Rak may be found at local pubs, restaurants, and bars.

algam Suyu: algam suyu is a distinct and distinct drink that originated in the adjacent city of Adana but is now extensively eaten in Antalya. It's a fermented drink prepared with turnips, red carrots, bulgur, salt, and water. Despite its brilliant purple color and strong perfume, algam suyu has a pleasant flavor with a mild tang. It is often served in large glasses and goes well with grilled meats, particularly at kebab places and traditional restaurants.

Salep: If you're in Antalya during the winter, don't pass up the chance to enjoy Salep, a delectable hot drink that has been adored for ages. Salep is created by combining pulverized tubers of wild orchids with hot milk, sugar, and a dash of cinnamon or nutmeg. The end product is a creamy, fragrant beverage that is both pleasant and calming. During the winter months, you may find Salep at traditional tea shops, cafés, and street sellers.

Turkish Tea (ay): No trip to Turkey is complete until you try the ubiquitous Turkish tea. Turkish tea, served in tiny tulip-shaped cups, is a strong black tea brewed in a unique two-chamber pot known as a "çaydanlk." The bottom chamber is filled with boiling water, while the top chamber is filled with loose tea leaves. Dilute the brewed tea with boiling water to your preferred flavor. Turkish tea is consumed throughout the day and is an important component of Turkish hospitality. Every corner in Antalya has tea shops, cafés, and street sellers selling çay.

Conclusion: Exploring Antalya's native beverages is an essential element of immersing oneself in the city's colorful culture and culinary traditions. There is something for every palette, whether you want refreshing non-alcoholic alternatives like Ayran and algam suyu or wish to enjoy the deep flavors of Rak or Salep. These drinks represent the region's history, customs, and the friendliness of the Turkish people. So, sample these local cocktails while in Antalya to round out your trip experience with a taste of true Mediterranean tastes.

- **STREET FOODS**

Lahmacun: Also known as Turkish pizza, lahmacun is a famous street cuisine in Antalya. A thin, crispy crust is covered with a savory blend of minced beef, onions, tomatoes, and herbs. After that, the lahmacun is cooked in a wood-fired oven, which gives it a delightful smokey taste. It is often served with fresh veggies and lemon wedges, which may be wrapped in the lahmacun and eaten like a wrap.

Döner Kebab: Döner kebab is a popular street meal in Turkey, including Antalya. This delectable cuisine is made up of marinated meat, generally beef or chicken that is placed on a vertical rotisserie and gently roasted. The meat is then thinly sliced and served on warm pita bread or wrapped with lettuce, tomatoes, onions, and a splash of sour yogurt sauce. Döner kebab is a must-try street cuisine in Antalya due to its delicate meat, fragrant spices, and fresh toppings.

Simit: Simit, often known as the Turkish bagel, is a popular street food snack in Turkey. It is a circular loaf that is coated with sesame seeds, which gives it a particular taste and texture. Simit is typically consumed for breakfast or as an afternoon snack. Street sellers serve freshly baked simit, which goes nicely with a cup of Turkish tea. It is a simple but tasty meal that you should not miss while in Antalya.

Midye Dolma: If you like seafood, try Midye Dolma, which translates as stuffed mussels. Fresh mussels are packed with a savory blend of rice, herbs, and spices in this street food specialty. After that, the mussels are cooked till soft and served with a touch of lemon. Midye Dolma is a famous Antalya street meal, frequently eaten as a fast and filling snack while walking along the coastal promenade.

Gözleme: Gözleme is a typical Turkish flatbread that may be filled with cheese, spinach, potatoes, or minced meat. The dough is thinly stretched out and griddle-cooked till golden brown and crispy. Gözleme is traditionally cooked by local ladies dressed in traditional attire and is a real gastronomic pleasure. Gözleme kiosks may be found in lively marketplaces where you can sample the unique tastes of this Turkish street cuisine.

Finally, enjoying Antalya's street foods is a fascinating experience that enables you to immerse yourself in local culture while indulging in delectable sensations. There are several street meals to sample, ranging from lahmacun and döner kebab to simit and Midye Dolma. So, when visiting this bustling Turkish city, be sure to explore the streets of Antalya and indulge in these delectable gastronomic treats.

Bruce Terry

CONCLUSION

In conclusion, the Antalya Travel Guide for the years 2023-2024 gives comprehensive and up-to-date information for everyone wishing to visit this magnificent city on the Turkish Riviera.

With its rich history, magnificent natural settings, and thriving cultural scene, Antalya provides a broad selection of attractions and activities for all sorts of tourists. From seeing historical ruins and archaeological sites to indulging in the local cuisine and enjoying the lovely beaches, travelers are promised an amazing experience. The brochure also emphasizes the city's increasing tourist infrastructure, including lodgings, transit choices, and suggested itineraries. Whether you are a history enthusiast, nature lover, or just seeking a tranquil holiday, the Antalya Travel Guide is a great resource for getting the most out of your trip to this wonderful area.

Printed in Great Britain
by Amazon